SUPREME COURT JUSTICES
EARL WARREN

Supreme Court Justices
Earl
Warren

Leslie Wolf Branscomb

Greensboro, North Carolina

SUPREME COURT JUSTICES

EARL WARREN
JOHN MARSHALL
THURGOOD MARSHALL
SONIA SOTOMAYOR

Supreme Court Justices: Earl Warren

Copyright © 2011 by Morgan Reynolds Publishing

Library of Congress Cataloging-in-Publication Data

Branscomb, Leslie Wolf.
 Supreme Court justices : Earl Warren / by Leslie Wolf Branscomb. -- 1st
ed.
     p. cm. -- (Supreme Court justices)
 Includes bibliographical references and index.
 ISBN 978-1-59935-158-2 (alk. paper)
 1. Warren, Earl, 1891-1974--Juvenile literature. 2. Judges--United
States--Biography--Juvenile literature. 3. United States. Supreme
Court--Biography--Juvenile literature. I. Title.
 KF8745.W3B73 2011
 347.73'2634--dc22
 [B]
                            2010020403

Printed in the United States of America
First Edition

To my father, Bob Wolf, whose sense of fairness and love of the law rivaled Earl Warren's

CONTENTS

Earl Warren at age eleven with his dog

A SON OF SCANDINAVIA

Earl Warren came from an unassuming background. The son of Scandinavian immigrants, he could have spent his life working on the railroad, as did his father and most of the men living in the small rough-and-tumble California town of Sumner in the early 1900s. Life was stark. Once, when Warren asked his father why he had no middle name his father answered, "My boy, when you were born I was too poor to give you a middle name." Warren could have settled for a humble life of hard work. Instead he lived an impressive life as a lawyer, prosecutor, governor, and chief justice of the Supreme Court.

Warren is widely considered to have changed the American social and legal landscape during his term on the bench. Which is not to say everyone loved him. As his Supreme Court career progressed, Warren's increasingly liberal positions were enough to cause the Republican president who'd appointed him, Dwight D. Eisenhower, to declare that giving Warren the chief justice's seat "was the biggest damn fool thing I ever did." But no amount of criticism ever deterred Warren from his goal of always doing what he felt was right. In sixteen years on the bench he presided over many cases that changed America forever, including rulings that banned racial segregation in schools, permitted interracial marriage, and defended the rights of accused criminals.

"My years on the Court were crowded with cases involving segregation, voting rights, and other civil rights, reapportionment of representative bodies, incursions on the Bill of Rights, and so forth—all of which had an emotional impact on large segments of the nation," Warren wrote in his memoirs. "Such cases would provoke controversy regardless of the way they might be decided. I, of course, understood that it was in the nature of the judicial process to evoke criticism because no judge can satisfy both sides, particularly in emotion-charged cases. Therefore, I never took objection to the criticism leveled at me or the Court, and made no attempt to justify publicly any of our decisions." This overwhelming desire to act fairly, to defend idealism and equality regardless of the consequences, was the hallmark of the Warren Court, and Warren's entire life.

Warren was born in Los Angeles, California, on March 19, 1891, to Methias H. Warren, a Norwegian immigrant, and Chrystal Hernlund Warren, who was from Sweden. He had one sibling, a sister named Ethel who was four years older.

Three-year-old Warren with his family

Methias Warren, who was also known as Matt, was born in Haugesund, a maritime city in southern Norway, where his family had a small farm. They emigrated to America when Methias was only a few months old, settling in Illinois and later moving to Iowa. From there Methias, as an adult, moved back to

Illinois, then to Minneapolis, Minnesota, and then made the move to the West Coast, first to San Diego, then Los Angeles. Warren's mother, Chrystal, was from Hälsingland, Sweden, and also came to the United States as an infant. Her family settled in Chicago, then moved to Minneapolis, where she met and married Methias at age eighteen.

Warren later said he never thought much about his ancestry until he entered politics. After he became the district attorney of Alameda County, genealogists came to him and urged him to have his "pedigree established for political purposes." A lawyer friend took it upon himself to trace Warren's ancestry, and told Warren he found him to be related to the first family of Warrens that had settled in Virginia when America was being colonized, and said he was also related to William the Conqueror of England. "This seemed a bit pompous and unlikely to me. I replied irreverently that he was risking great danger because if he went back much further he might find his ancestors and mine hanging from palm trees and throwing coconuts at each other. This outraged him, and I am not sure that he ever forgave me." What the would-be researcher didn't know was that Warren's original family name was the Norwegian name Varran, which had only been anglicized in the last couple of generations, as often happened with immigrants in those days.

Warren's father was a longtime employee of the Southern Pacific Railroad, where he worked as a railroad car inspector and repairman. But he lost his job with the railroad after he joined the failed strike against the company in 1894. The strike was bitter, and when it ended, the men who left their jobs to strike were blacklisted and not allowed to return to the company. So Methias Warren moved to San Bernardino without his wife and children to take a job on the Santa Fe Railroad. After a time he was taken back by Southern Pacific to work in Bakersfield, which was then called Kern City, in central California. The rest of the family joined Methias and moved to the little town of Sumner nearby.

Sumner had a population of only a few hundred people until oil was discovered. The resulting boom upped the population to about 1,300. The town was built around the railroad. Some families lived there, but many of the men who worked on the railroad were boarders who stayed temporarily in the hotels and rooming houses, moving from town to town as work became available.

Earl attended Baker Street School, Washington Junior High School, and Kern County Union High School (which is now called Bakersfield High School).

Around the turn of the century Sumner was little more than a dusty frontier railroad town. It was extremely hot and dry there, and for most of the year every time the wind started up there were terrible dust storms that lasted for days. The dust seeped through every crevice of the houses until sometimes residents felt as if they might suffocate. The springtime brought a brief respite, however, and for a few weeks the town and surrounding area was full of golden poppy blooms, blue lupines and other wildflowers.

The Warren family went on walks to collect flowers, and Earl remembered his father once remarked, "The Lord must have intended these hills for something more than these flowers for such a few days each year." He was right—in 1899 oil was discovered there, and irrigation later turned Bakersfield into a booming agricultural hub.

But during Earl's youth the town existed for no reason other than to support the railroad. There were few cultural facilities or social activities.

A photograph of the first, second, and third grades at the Baker Street School in East Bakersfield, California. Warren, in the first grade at the time, is in the front row, seventh from the left, wearing a Lord Fauntleroy suit and curls in his hair.

There was a Methodist church, a lodge, and several saloons, but no theater or library. Social life centered around the railroad station and townspeople gathered there to visit and see if they knew anyone arriving on the evening passenger trains from Los Angeles and San Francisco. The trains always stopped in Sumner for servicing and a change of crews, during which time the passengers disembarked and mingled with the townsfolk. There were three sets of people living in Sumner at the time: the first were the railroad workers, who tended to live north of the tracks, and the second were the Basque or French shepherds who lived south of the tracks and drove their flocks into the mountains each spring. The two groups didn't associate much, and their only mutual contact was through the children, who all attended the one school in town. The third group was the Chinese railroad laborers, all men without families who lived in railroad barracks and didn't associate with the other residents.

As a boy Earl had many pets: dogs, sheep, rabbits, chickens, and even an eagle. His favorite was his burro named Jack, who was his friend and companion for many years. With Jack, he rode around the countryside to go swimming, fishing or chasing jackrabbits and squirrels.

Jack later died of poisoning, most likely at the hands of disgruntled neighbors who complained repeatedly about the animal's constant braying.

Earl admitted he wasn't a very good student, although he did well in the subjects that interested him such as history, French, and English. He said that while in school he was not interested in girls, and they were patronizing to him, probably because of his small stature—he did not begin to really grow until he was in the eleventh grade. He played the clarinet both in his school band and the town orchestra, and joined the newly formed musicians' union at age fifteen. There were sixteen students in Earl's high-school graduating class, and he was one of only four who went to college.

During his senior year Earl was selected to play the lead part in his class play. However, rehearsal ran past midnight one night, and he and two other boys who were also in the play slept in the next morning and arrived late for their graduation rehearsal. The principal accused the three of trying to sabotage the rehearsal, and expelled them from school. At a hastily called meeting of the board of education, the boys were reinstated, and both the play and graduation went on as planned. Years later, Warren found it amusing that the same board of education chose to honor him by naming a school building after him.

Even though he was an avid sportsman in later years, as a youth Earl did not participate in organized sports except for a brief time on the high-school baseball team during his senior year. He lost his spot on the team, however, due to the requirements of all his outside jobs.

Methias Warren emphasized the importance of hard work to his son, and young Earl worked summers on a railroad crew during his teenage years as a railroad "call boy," whose job was to ensure that members of the train crew were on hand and ready for their regular runs, and any extra runs. He also worked at the railroad as a "freight hustler," loading and handling freight. His father always made him promise that at summer's end he would return to school, because he didn't want Earl ending up like so many other young men in town, working for the railroad his entire life. "He often reminded me of a saying about railroading: 'You cuss it every day, but once in it you can't get out even if you try,'" Warren recalled.

He did other odd jobs as well in his youth, including working as a bakery wagon driver, a farm hand, and a cub reporter for the Bakersfield *Californian* newspaper. He also for a time delivered blocks of ice to homes. Considering there was no air conditioning and summer temperatures in the Central Valley were often more than one hundred degrees, he considered this job almost a humanitarian service. He did all these things to earn money for college, and these experiences, particularly working on the railroad, helped him learn the value of hard work and the rough life of the poor working class.

> I witnessed crime and vice of all kinds countenanced by corrupt government . . . I saw men rush from the pay car to the gambling houses and never leave until they had lost every cent of their month's laborious earnings . . . I saw conditions in many of the homes where the breadwinner had lost his earnings at the gaming tables. I became familiar with the ten and even twelve-hour day, seven days a week. I worked many such hours myself.

Looking back on his early life in later years, Warren concluded that those years also prepared him for the less pleasant realities of politics and law. "The things I learned about monopolistic power, political dominance, corruption in government, and their effect on the people of a community were valuable lessons that would tend to shape my career throughout life, although I did not then foresee any such results."

A Legal Career Interrupted

After graduating from high school, Warren worked for two months on the railroad, and then in August boarded a train bound for the University of California in Berkeley, which was then known simply as the University of California, since it was the only campus in the state. Warren couldn't have imagined at the time that he would later help establish the University of California system, with its many campuses. He didn't know much about the school when he embarked on the long, hot train trip in 115-degree weather, but his family had decided it was the best college for him to attend.

Since both oil and gold were being mined in Kern County, Warren's father thought that studying mining engineering would provide his son with a good profession. Warren had never been away from home before. When he left, his father didn't offer much in the way of parting advice, but said simply, "Well, my boy, you are going away from home. You are a man now, and I am sure you are going to act like one."

Warren was surprised his father did not realize he had no aptitude for mechanical things, let alone engineering. At some point, while on the journey to the Bay Area and without really having any good reason to do so, Warren decided to major in law instead. His change of heart may have been related to his experiences watching courtroom trials as a boy. Sometimes, when he rode his bicycle past the town courthouse on the way home from school, Warren stopped and went inside to watch trials. He was impressed by the lawyers and admired their public speaking abilities.

Warren's train arrived first in Oakland, near Berkeley. He caught a ferry across the bay to San Francisco, having decided to spend a night in the grand old city. However, he found it a "sad sight to behold," since not much rebuilding had taken place since the devastating earthquake and fire of 1906 three years earlier. The downtown was a mass of rubble, with burnt-out buildings standing like skeletons in the middle.

Upon arriving at the university the next day, Warren went to the La Junta Club, a fraternal organization, on the recommendation of a family friend who was a member. The members invited Warren to stay for dinner, and during the meal he regaled the other young men with tales of his high

Memorial Glade and Sather Tower on the campus of the University of California, Berkeley

school high jinks, and of how he and the other boys would try to outwit the principal, whom they considered mean and unfair.

When he finished telling his story, no one said anything more about it at dinner. Later that night, one of the seniors invited Warren to have dinner with him the following week in Oakland. At that dinner, the senior sternly but kindly lectured an embarrassed Warren, and told him things were not done that way at the university. The upperclassman told Warren that the students were on the honor system and expected to maintain high standards and behave respectably at all times. Despite the warning, Warren was invited a few weeks later to join the club, becoming its only freshman member.

Warren was modest about his accomplishments at the university, claiming there were few. "I must admit that I was not a serious student. I was more concerned with adequacy than profundity. I was more interested in the university as a community of lively, stimulating people than as a community of scholars," he wrote in his memoirs.

> It was a whole new world for me, a wonderful new world—large, dynamic, enthusiastic, friendly, and with unlimited freedom. Coming from our relatively isolated little railroad town to this vibrant community was a revelation, and moving from a graduating high school class of sixteen seniors to a record college freshman class of over nine hundred from all over the world was almost overwhelming.

For recreation, Warren played his clarinet occasionally for dances, and spent time playing cards and drinking beer at a German restaurant near campus. He also joined Skull and Keys, another fraternal organization, where the members held meetings, read books, produced an annual play and, of course, drank beer. "All of this may sound as though beer was a major factor in my college life, though in reality it was not," Warren wrote in his memoirs. "None of these fellowships was dissolute in any sense, but I must confess to having had a great liking for the companionship of students who liked to eat together, read together, and visit over a glass or two." Warren so enjoyed fraternity life that he and his La Junta Club brothers applied for a charter to become part of the Sigma Phi society, and were accepted.

Warren claims he barely passed trigonometry—to fail would have meant not graduating—and even years later he still had nightmares about taking the final exam.

He graduated in 1912 with a bachelor of letters degree in legal studies. He went on to study for his law degree at the university's Boalt Hall School of Law. While in law school he also worked at a law office in Berkeley to gain extra experience. Doing so was considered a violation of the law school's rules governing student behavior, but Warren apparently felt so strongly that he needed to gain some practical experience, he considered it a calculated risk. He graduated with his law degree, or L.L.B. as it was then called, in 1914, and was admitted to the state bar the same year he earned his law degree. In those years, no lengthy bar examination was required; admission to the bar was earned upon the recommendation of a member of the law school's faculty.

Warren's father expected him to return to Bakersfield to practice law, but after having lived in Berkeley and seen San Francisco, Warren couldn't imagine moving back to the hot, dusty Central Valley town. He took his first job as a lawyer with an oil company in San Francisco, Associated Oil Company. It was a post he held for only a year. Warren described his boss at the oil company as an irascible old man, who often sent Warren out to buy cigars for him, and treated him without dignity. When Warren quit, without another job lined up, his boss demanded to know why. Warren told him he was unhappy working there and felt he had been treated poorly. The boss then said, "'I have had probably fifty young men work for me, and none of them ever expressed such dissatisfaction.' I was bold enough to tell him that if he had treated them differently perhaps he would have needed only one instead of the fifty." Just before leaving the oil firm, Warren was sent to obtain an order from the chief justice of the California Supreme Court. He was impressed and uplifted by the way the man greeted him cordially and with courtesy, and vowed that if he ever had an office of his own, he would treat every visitor in the same courteous manner.

Warren spent a couple years in private practice, working for a law firm in Oakland, Robinson & Robinson. He joined the Young Lawyers' Club of Alameda County, eventually becoming its vice president. Warren, two other young lawyers and a senior lawyer, decided to start their own legal practice together and were searching for office space when their careers were interrupted by World War I.

In the spring of 1917, Warren volunteered to join the U.S. Army as an officer, applying for admission to the First Officers Training Camp. There were more applicants than spaces, and he was rejected. He subsequently was assigned as a draftee to the Ninety-first Division at Camp Lewis, Washington.

Conditions at the camp were dismal. They spent the first weeks wearing the same clothes they arrived in, and living in squalor until their uniforms arrived. Much of their time was spent in quarantine for the first four months, because they had no decent clothing, and there were bouts of spinal meningitis and measles in the camp. They had no rifles, so they trained with wood cut into the shape of rifles. They didn't even have a pistol to signal the start of a track meet. Warren was named first sergeant, a post for which he felt unqualified, since he had managed to skip the required ROTC training at Berkeley by playing clarinet in the university's military band. Warren was finally accepted for an officers' training camp in January, 1918.

Warren spent his entire military service in the U.S., never shipping out to the battles taking places overseas. At one point, he and his fellow officer trainees were put on a cross-country train, and they hoped they were being sent to France. However, they were sent to Camp Lee in Petersburg, Virginia, where they were assigned to train troops as replacements for soldiers returning from overseas. It was a long, hot, miserable summer during which many men suffered heat prostration. They had only thirty days to train the young men who arrived for battle, even though many of them had never before fired a rifle, and quite a number didn't even know how to read or write. A few times the young officers took a recreational visit to nearby historic Richmond, where they were shocked to see the city decorated with Confederate flags, with not an American flag in sight, even though the Civil War had ended more than fifty years earlier.

In September 1918 Camp Lee was hit by the Spanish influenza epidemic, which ended up killing more people than died in World Wars I and II combined. Thousands at the camp were sickened and many died, although Warren was not afflicted. Around that time Warren was promoted to first lieutenant and ordered to Camp McArthur in Waco, Texas, to serve as a bayonet instructor. He arrived there on November 9, 1918. Two days later the armistice was signed and the war came to an end. He was discharged from the Army a month later.

Warren resumed his legal career, although he didn't know what had become of the two other lawyers he'd planned to open an office with, since they'd also joined the armed forces during the war. So he took a job as a clerk for the Assembly Judiciary Committee of the California legislature in 1919. Later that year he became a deputy city attorney for the city of Oakland, prosecuting criminal cases.

In 1920 he became a deputy assistant for the district attorney of Alameda

A platoon during training

County, which includes the cities of Oakland, Alameda, and Berkeley. He worked for the district attorney's office for the next eighteen years.

As a young prosecutor he displayed some of the work habits that led him to success in later years. He often worked until midnight, mastering his own cases and helping on cases assigned to others. There wasn't much turnover in the district attorney's office until the 1920s, when the practice of law became more profitable in Oakland and senior attorneys began to leave. Warren made a point of assisting other lawyers on their cases:

> It was exciting for me, every day of it, and I made quick progress. Whenever one of the old-timers would leave, Mr. Decoto (the District Attorney) would ask the chief deputy, "Who knows anything about his cases?" and the deputy would often reply, "Warren has been helping him." The district attorney would then say, "Well, let's turn his work over to Warren." I worked practically every day of the week and ordinarily five nights.

His diligence and attention to detail, more than his legal expertise, eventually helped Warren become a great Supreme Court justice. Five years after joining the office, in January 1925, he was appointed to the position of Alameda County district attorney, to fill the unexpired term of his predecessor, Ezra Decoto, who resigned to take a position as railroad commissioner.

Despite his now-lofty position and new responsibilities, work wasn't the only thing on Warren's mind that year, and his thoughts soon turned to marriage.

Governor Earl Warren with his wife, Nina Meyers Warren, in 1943

The Warren family in Oakland, California, in 1942

MARRIAGE AND FAMILY

Warren went to dances and parties, but did not date women very frequently. About a year after joining the district attorney's office, he was invited to a summertime birthday swim party at the Piedmont Baths in Oakland. There he met Nina Elisabeth Palmquist Meyers, the daughter of a Swedish Baptist minister. Like Warren's mother, she too came from Sweden as a child. When they met, Nina was twenty-eight years old and was already a widow with a three-year-old son, James. She and her son were living with her widowed stepmother. Nina was supporting the three of them by working as the manager of a women's specialty shop in Oakland.

During their courtship, they often went out to dinner and to see a show at the theater on Saturday evenings. It wasn't long before they began talking about marriage, but Warren wanted to wait until he was earning more money and could support a family. At the time, he was working as a deputy district attorney, and making about $250 a month.

When he was appointed district attorney in January 1925, they decided to marry. By then they had been seeing each other for about four years. But the nuptials were delayed for a variety of reasons, including

The Fairmont Empress Hotel, where the Warrens stayed during their honeymoon, in British Colombia, Canada

Warren's mother's eye surgery and her subsequent illness. As soon as Chrystal Warren was well enough, the couple was married, on October 14, 1925, in a quiet family service at a Baptist church. Though they tried to keep the ceremony a secret, two friends of Warren's found out about their application for a marriage license and arranged for the entire fleet of the county highway patrol to escort the couple from the church.

With sirens blaring, the motorcycle officers escorted Warren and his bride in their black Buick to the county line, where they continued northward to their two-week honeymoon in British Columbia, Canada. They stayed at the grand Empress Hotel on Vancouver Island. Warren thought the island, with its abundant flowers and greenery, was lovely, but the weather was "atrocious." It rained constantly for days, so for entertainment, Warren took his new bride to see a British-style trial. One of Warren's enduring memories of his honeymoon is of watching that trial, in which a Chinese immigrant was accused of shooting and attempting to kill his wife's lover. The man was acquitted.

Warren adopted Nina's son from her first marriage. The couple eventually had five more children of their own, in little more than six

years: Virginia, Earl Jr., Dorothy, Nina Elisabeth, and Robert. He, his wife, and the children were often pictured together publicly over the years, and made an ideal family.

Now that Warren had a grand salary of $7,200 a year, he bought a seven-bedroom, three-story home in Oakland for his growing family. He bought it already furnished, and wouldn't have been able to afford it had he not purchased it from a banker who had fallen on hard times. For fun, the children often joined Warren on his evening forays to his favorite bookstore in Oakland. They also enjoyed visiting the zoo, taking the ferry to San Francisco, and occasionally venturing into Chinatown for dinner at a Chinese restaurant. Warren never brought his work home, because he didn't want to expose his impressionable young children to the violence and crime that was part of his job as a prosecutor.

Family life suited him well, and his wife Nina was a great supporter of Warren's ambitions. His loyalty to his wife ran deep over the course of their forty-nine-year marriage. Just before his death, Warren dedicated his memoirs to "Nina, the best thing that ever happened to me."

Elementary school students stand to recite the Pledge of Allegiance before an American flag in a classroom.

A SUCCESSFUL PROSECUTOR

Warren excelled in his job as the district attorney of Alameda County, and was reelected to the post three times, in 1926, 1930, and 1934. During his years as a prosecutor he earned a reputation for being no-nonsense and tough on crime. He was also known to be tough on his employees, a taskmaster who expected everyone to work the same long hours that he did. He rarely expressed gratitude or thanks to his subordinates for their hard work, since he simply expected as much. At times his critics thought he was high-handed and even arrogant, but always fair. None of the convictions he won as a prosecutor were ever overturned on appeal.

Even then, some of his decisions showed the jurist he would become, such as when he fought for criminal defendants to have court-appointed lawyers—even though Warren's job was to prosecute them, he still felt any indigent accused of a crime was entitled to a decent defense. He fought for and succeeded in changing the county charter to include a provision to provide a public defender for all indigent defendants. He also joined with some other lawyers to open a Legal Aid Bureau in Oakland and paid its expenses for a few years to help the bureau become established.

Even though he had reputation as a crime-fighter, Warren didn't actually find any thrill in sending people to prison. While he took satisfaction in a job well done by his office, he always worried about the fallout, and particularly disliked death penalty cases.

> It was never only the culprit who suffered. There were invariably an innocent mother or father, wife, children, brothers or sisters who were affected perhaps more than the defendant himself. And then there were the murder cases. I never heard a jury foreman say, 'Guilty of murder in the first degree' without having a feeling of nausea. The taking of human life, even by the law in retribution for an unlawful killing is so awesome and gruesome that it becomes a traumatic experience for any participant in the legal tragedy.

His career continued to soar. A 1931 nationwide survey named Warren the best district attorney in the country. Warren became more involved in politics, chairing the California Republican party from 1934 through 1936. He was a Republican national committeeman when he ran for state attorney general in 1938, at the age of forty-seven. At the time he was running for attorney general, his politics were considerably more conservative than they became in later years. During the race, Warren favored legislation that made it mandatory for schoolchildren to salute the flag. He also proclaimed that the Communist Party should not be entitled to legal recognition in the United States. Neither of those positions would have led anyone to suspect that the same man would later, as chief justice of the Supreme Court, rule that children could not be forced to pray in school, and that a suspected Communist sympathizer should not be compelled to name his cohorts in court.

He won the election, becoming the twentieth attorney general of the state of California.

However, during the campaign Warren's father Methias was murdered in his own home. Warren was speaking to a Masonic gathering at the Claremont Hotel in Berkeley on May 15, 1938, when a telegram arrived informing him of the murder, which took place the night before. Methias Warren, who was then seventy-one years old, was beaten with a metal pipe while sitting at his kitchen table. The house was ransacked.

By then, Warren's parents had been separated for more than a decade. His mother, Chrystal, had moved out during the late 1920s and settled in Oakland, to be near their daughter Ethel. The fact of his parents' separation was embarrassing to Warren, and he tried for decades to conceal the truth, even telling people at the time of the killing that his mother was not there when it happened because she was away in Oakland undergoing eye surgery for cataracts.

Although several people were questioned in connection with the murder, the case was never solved. Police speculated that Methias may have known his killer, but nothing was ever proved conclusively. The press speculated that the elder Warren may have been murdered by someone bent on causing harm or getting even with his son Earl. While talking to the press that night, uncharacteristically, Warren broke down and cried. A photographer took his picture. It was a different era, however, when politicians were often shielded from having their weaknesses exposed to the public, and the other reporters present demanded the photographer remove the film from his camera and destroy it, which he did.

The tragic event had a huge impact on Warren's life; nevertheless, he still stood up for the rights of accused criminals throughout his legal career. The tragedy did not turn Warren into an angry, bitter man bent on revenge.

Warren won the election and was sworn in on January 3, 1939. He did well as attorney general and is remembered for helping modernize the office during his term. Among his accomplishments as attorney general, he is credited with organizing state law enforcement officials into regions. He also led a statewide anti-crime effort and was known for fighting organized crime. Warren undertook raids on gambling dens and cracked down on illegal gambling ships operating off the coast of Southern California—his zeal for attacking gambling operations was no doubt fueled by the stark experiences of his youth, where he saw men working on the railroad gamble away their pay, leaving their families destitute.

There was one major black mark on his record as attorney general of California: his support of the internment of Japanese-Americans in California during World War II. At the time, Warren's beliefs echoed those of many Americans, who feared the Japanese following the bombing of U.S. forces in Pearl Harbor, Hawaii.

The USS *Arizona* sinking in Pearl Harbor, Hawaii, after the Japanese attacked on December 7, 1941

On December 7, 1941, the Japanese Navy struck the U.S. naval base in Honolulu with surprising force, launching the United States into World War II. The Japanese attacked with 350 airplanes, sinking or damaging 188 U.S. aircraft, eight Navy battleships, and six other ships, as the U.S. servicemen scrambled to defend themselves. In all, 2,403 Americans were killed, including civilians, and 1,178 were wounded. Before the attack on Pearl Harbor, many in the U.S. didn't want to get involved in the war, which was being fought primarily in Europe. The bombing and the mass casualties, however, galvanized people and outraged the public. Animosity toward the Japanese was widespread.

California was the hub of the aircraft industry, producing airplanes and ships for the military. The state's leaders felt it was imperative that warship and plane production be maintained, and feared the factories would be sabotaged by Japanese people living in California who were secretly spies or sympathizers with their countrymen. The public's fear of the Japanese became extreme, and included paranoia against even those people of Japanese extraction who were born and raised in the United States. There were then more than 100,000 people living in California who claimed at least some Japanese blood. Two-thirds of them were American citizens. There was violence against the Japanese residents as the fear and anger mounted.

Due to the terror and prejudice that overwhelmed the country and particularly California, about 112,000 people of Japanese ancestry living near the West Coast were rounded up and made to live in internment camps farther inland. Thousands lost their homes and businesses as a result, when they were moved to camps for the duration of the war.

now that our state would have reaped great benefits from it," Warren wrote in his memoirs. "No state had such a program, and yet I believed something of this kind was inevitable." But the concept of government-mandated insurance was so shockingly liberal for a Republican governor that some people even denounced it as socialism. The American Medical Association attacked the proposal and it was subsequently rejected by the state legislature.

In 1947 Warren signed a law repealing school segregation statutes in the California education code, after the state Supreme Court upheld a lower court's ruling banning segregation in schools, foreshadowing his later leadership in desegregating schools nationwide.

He was considered a very successful governor, a perception that was no doubt aided by the fact that California and the nation were experiencing a prosperous post-war period. The booming economy allowed the governor and legislature to increase state expenditures and lower taxes. Warren was reelected a second time in 1950, even though his opponent was James Roosevelt, the son of the late President Franklin D. Roosevelt. He faced an opponent with a surname that was known nationwide, yet Warren won by a million votes, becoming the first and only California governor to serve three terms in office. (A term-limit law was enacted in 1990, and now California governors may serve no more than two four-year terms in office.)

With his political fortunes continuing to rise, Warren was courted repeatedly for national office. There was talk as early as 1944 that he might run for president. In 1948 the Republican Party nominated him to run for the office of vice president on a ticket with New York governor Thomas E. Dewey. He was chosen for "geopolitical" reasons—the Republicans hoped Warren, the popular governor of California, would appeal to voters on the West Coast. President Harry S. Truman

Harry Truman, the thirty-third president of the United States

Senator Richard Nixon, who would later become the thirty-seventh president of the United States

was unpopular and deemed unlikely to be reelected. The Democrats seemed to be in disarray, and the Republican ticket seemed poised to enjoy an easy victory. However, it was not to be. That fall Warren suffered the first election defeat of his career, when he and Dewey lost to Truman and Vice President Alben W. Barkley.

Despite that loss, by 1952 Warren was widely considered the Republicans' favorite for nomination for president of the United States. Warren was selected to lead the California delegation to the Republican Convention that year, where the nominees for president and vice president would be chosen. The convention did not go well for Warren, however. A political struggle with U.S. Senator Richard M. Nixon (who became president some years later), was the start of a tense relationship between the two.

At the convention, Nixon was a delegate who was pledged to vote for Warren as the Republican nominee, reflecting the wishes of his constituents. However, Nixon could barely conceal his preference for the other Republican candidate, General Dwight D. Eisenhower. Seeing the writing on the wall, Warren withdrew his name from consideration and threw his support behind Eisenhower, who then picked Nixon as his vice-presidential running mate. Eisenhower and Nixon went on to win the election that year. As a result, Eisenhower owed Warren a favor.

The animosity between Nixon and Warren continued for years. In 1957, after Nixon was vice president and Warren was chief justice, Warren refused an invitation to attend the American Bar Association's convention if Nixon was going to be there. The Bar Association chose not to invite the vice president, giving a fairly clear indication of the two men's relative standing in the legal community.

Dwight Eisenhower, the thirty-fourth president

President Eisenhower, smiling and waving, with his wife in the back seat, and Warren in the front passenger seat, after the election

SUPER CHIEF

t wasn't long before Eisenhower had the opportunity to repay Warren for his support. In exchange for helping Eisenhower secure the Republican presidential nomination, Eisenhower promised Warren the first open seat on the Supreme Court. Warren construed that to mean any open seat would be his, even the post of chief justice. Eisenhower later wrote in his memoirs that he mentioned the possibility of a Supreme Court post to Warren but didn't consider the possibility that the first vacant seat might be that of the chief justice. In 1953, the year after Eisenhower was elected president, Warren announced that he intended to step down from the governor's job. Shortly afterward, Supreme Court Chief Justice Fred M. Vinson died unexpectedly.

Warren had already accepted an offer to become the solicitor general of the U.S. Department of Justice, which handles the litigation on behalf of the United States before the Supreme Court. Eisenhower reportedly first offered the seat to John Foster Dulles, the U.S. secretary of state, but Dulles declined. Thomas Dewey, the former presidential candidate, also turned down the opportunity. Eisenhower also considered appointing one of the existing associate justices on the Supreme Court, but was pressured by his political party to appoint a prominent Republican. Some thought it likely that Vice President Nixon and a U.S. Senator, William Knowland, pressured Eisenhower to appoint Warren to the Court just to get Warren out of California politics. Warren by then had reminded Eisenhower of his earlier promise.

Despite lacking any experience as a judge, Warren was appointed to the post of chief justice by Eisenhower on October. 2, 1953, sworn in three days later, and began actively presiding over the court almost immediately. At first, because he was not familiar with the procedures of the Court, he asked the senior associate justice, Hugo Black, to preside until he could familiarize himself with his new duties. It only took Warren a few weeks to get up to speed.

The Supreme Court, in addition to occupying a grand structure on Capitol Hill, is a place full of history, where certain traditions are always observed. Warren was awed by the building and everything it stood for. Built between 1932 and 1935, the gleaming white courthouse is ninety-two feet high and constructed with marble from Vermont, Georgia, Alabama, Spaint, Italy, and Africa. It has a gilded ceiling and the wooden judges' bench is of dark mahogany from Honduras. When it first opened, not everyone appreciated the grand new building. Associate Justice Harlan Fiske Stone, who later became chief justice, called it "almost bombastically pretentious . . . wholly inappropriate for a quiet group of old boys such as the Supreme Court." Warren, however, felt the courthouse was beautiful.

It is indeed an awesome sight as one stands before its Grecian serenity and reads the words chiseled in white marble above the main entrance. Like the building itself, the words are inspiring. They say: "Equal Justice Under Law." As one enters through the massive bronze doors and passes down a lofty hallway to the courtroom around which the building was designed, a feeling of solemnity and a sense of history build until the visitor arrives at the Supreme Court room itself. Inside, the stately side columns of Italian marble, the polished mahogany furnishings and the red velour hangings induce a self-imposed, respectful silence.

The U.S. Supreme Court

There was opposition to Warren's appointment—more than two hundred objections to Warren's nomination had been filed. By then some of his more left-leaning decisions as governor had been noticed by hard-line conservatives, who called Warren a "Marxist"—a reference to Karl Marx, a German philosopher and socialist revolutionary. Marx, who lived in the 1800s and died seven years before Warren was born, was best known for creating an anti-capitalist political philosophy. He was the author of a controversial political manuscript called *The Communist Manifesto*, which laid out the philosophy and purposes of the Communist Party.

At the time of Warren's confirmation hearing, in the 1950s in the United States, calling someone a Marxist was a serious insult. Paranoia about suspected members and activities of the Communist party was widespread at the time, fueled in part by Americans' fears of a war with Russia, which was governed by Communists. Warren declined an invitation to appear at the Senate confirmation hearings. During the hearings right-wing groups testified against him, saying he allowed crime to flourish in California. And there was also the concern—echoed by many—that Warren had no judicial experience. His appointment as the nation's fourteenth chief justice of the United States was nevertheless formally confirmed by the Senate on March 1, 1954. He was the last chief justice born in the nineteenth century.

Eisenhower defended his appointment of Warren, in the face of critics who said he wasn't qualified because he'd never served as a judge. Author and diplomat Nicholas Roosevelt, a distant cousin of presidents Theodore and Franklin D. Roosevelt, sent a letter to Eisenhower's younger brother saying that Warren's legal experience was scant and nothing in his background qualified him for the post of chief justice.

Upon hearing of this, the president wrote to his brother, Milton Stover Eisenhower, defending his choice. The letter, dated October 9, 1953, refers to Roosevelt's missive:

> The writer of the letter apparently assumes that a life-time on the bench or in the exclusive practice of law would produce the highest possible qualification for the Supreme Court. I disagree . . . I believe that we need statesmanship on the Supreme Court. Statesmanship is developed in the hard knocks of a general experience, private and public.

> Naturally, a man occupying the post must be competent in the law—and Warren has had seventeen years of practice in public law, during which his record was one of remarkable accomplishment and success, to say nothing of dedication. He has been very definitely a liberal-conservative; he represents the kind of political, economic, and social thinking that I believe we need on the Supreme Court. Finally, he has a national name for integrity, uprightness, and courage that, again, I believe we need on the Court.

Eisenhower was later sorely disappointed when Warren made his mark on the Court with a series of highly controversial rulings which showed him to be much more liberal than Eisenhower expected. This was the point at which Eisenhower uttered the often-repeated words, declaring his appointment of Warren to be "the biggest damn fool thing I ever did."

When Warren joined the Court, the justices were divided between those who favored judicial activism, as Warren did, and those who advocated judicial restraint. Warren demonstrated great skill at "massing the court," or persuading the justices to stand as one even on controversial decisions. It didn't take long for Warren to establish himself.

His affable demeanor helped him successfully forge consensus on the Court in many controversial cases over his sixteen-year tenure. As Justice Potter Stewart later said, "he possessed instinctive qualities of leadership." According to Stewart, Warren didn't lead by his intellect. "But he was an instinctive leader whom you respected and for whom you had affection and . . . as the presiding member of our conference he was just ideal."

Associate Justice William J. Brennan Jr. described Warren kindly:

> (He was) physically a large man, naturally gregarious and open, with a warm and engaging smile. It was impossible to dislike him. He liked people and people liked him. He was instinctively courteous and sensitive to the feelings of others. He put strangers at their ease immediately. However great their judicial differences with him, his brethren (sixteen Associate Justices during his tenure) without exception personally were very fond of him.

Warren was a big and imposing man, with blonde hair and intense blue eyes, as befitting his Scandinavian heritage. He stood a little over six feet tall and weighed more than two hundred pounds. He was known for his broad smile, hearty handshake and cordial manners, and quite often wore double-breasted suits made of blue serge. He knew hundreds of people by name, but did not have very many close friends, preferring to spend time with his family.

A *New York Times* article likewise described Warren as "a mild and genial man" who got along well with his colleagues on the Court. "Members of the Court often engaged in vigorous disagreements over issues, but their personal relations were always cordial," the reporter wrote. Justice Felix Frankfurter, who was already on the Supreme Court when Warren was named chief justice, was the one who most often disagreed with Warren on issues of law. Frankfurter was reputed to possess the sharpest legal mind among the men. He favored judicial restraint, instead of the activism for which Warren had become known, and would often vigorously oppose Warren on such cases, with the exception of those involving racial segregation, where the two saw eye-to-eye. Frankfurter considered Warren a mere politician; Warren, for his part, was irritated by Frankfurter's frequent memos attempting to instruct him in the proper role of the Court.

A 1962 group portrait of the United States Supreme Court Justices in their robes, in Washington, D.C. Standing, from the left: Associate Justices Byron White, William J. Brennan Jr., Potter Stewart, and Arthur Goldberg. Sitting, from the left: Associate Justices Tom Clark, Hugo Black, Chief Justice Earl Warren, William O Douglas, and John Marshall Harlan

The Warren years were marked by numerous cases in which the Court took on the defense of individual rights. Warren considered this a proper role for the Court, and he never saw his role as being that of a passive observer. He would often interrupt lawyers arguing their cases before the court to ask them, "Yes, but is it fair?" While on the Supreme Court, Warren earned an affectionate nickname from his fans: "Super Chief."

Yet Warren's decisions also earned him some animosity from the public, especially those who disagreed with his more progressive positions. Conservatives called for his impeachment. All this animosity was aimed at a man whom many believe committed no greater crime than to drag the Supreme Court into the modern age. He is often credited with being the first justice to actually apply the constitution to the lives of regular folks. The Bill of Rights had existed for many years, but often states were left to interpret its meaning, as the Court generally declined to meddle in states' affairs before Warren was seated. In particular, the Fourteenth Amendment, adopted in 1858, stated that all persons born in the United States were citizens and therefore guaranteed equal protection of the laws. However, that wasn't the case for African Americans living in the southern states in the 1950s. Segregation was the norm, and African Americans enjoyed nothing close to equality in the courts, let alone on buses, in restaurants, and in schools. This, above all, was the first thing Warren chose to rectify.

Soldiers from the 101st Airborne Division escort the Little Rock Nine students into the all-white Central High School in Little Rock, Arkansas.

James Meredith walking to class at the University of Mississippi, accompanied by U.S. marshals

AN END TO SEGREGATION

The case that made the biggest splash during Warren's tenure on the Court was *Brown v. Board of Education*. It outlawed school segregation, and this bold decision is considered by many historians to be the event that kicked off the civil rights protests and ensuing changes of the 1950s and 1960s. The turbulent South was particularly riled by the decision. Nevertheless, all the civil rights laws passed by Congress in the wake of the *Brown* case were unanimously upheld by the Warren Court.

Oliver Brown, the father of Linda Brown, sued the Topeka, Kansas, board of education for his daughter's right to go to an all-white school near her home. Because of the segregation rules that were common at the time, however, Linda and her sister had to walk through a dangerous railroad switch yard to get to the bus stop that took them to another school farther from their home, where "colored" children attended.

The case was originally argued in December, 1952. Chief Justice Vinson, Warren's predecessor, was in favor of continuing school segregation based on the doctrine of "separate but equal" that was established in an earlier 1896 case, in which the Supreme Court allowed segregation on trains and in public schools. The Court ordered rearguments on some points of the case in December, 1953.

At the time Warren arrived on the Court, the justices were split. Even those who opposed racial segregation in schools believed that the Court may not have the authority to overturn it. Warren was being cautious as well, mindful that he was not yet formally confirmed by the U.S. Senate, and that the senators from the still-segregated southern states had a say in whether he remained as chief justice. He let his opinion be known to his colleagues shortly after the first oral argument, that racial segregation could not be sustained unless one assumed blacks were inferior to whites, a concept he did not support. Throughout the winter of 1953 and early 1954 the justices talked over the case, and eventually Warren won each one of them over to his point of view.

With Warren as its new leader, in May of 1954 the court announced that it found unanimously that separate educational facilities for blacks and whites were inherently unequal, and that segregation denied African Americans equal protection under the law. While the case was won based on the Fourteenth Amendment right to equal protection, legal scholars later said the decision was based more on Warren's fundamental belief in right and wrong than on the constitutional issues at hand. This would come to be a trademark of the Warren Court: some felt that Warren was far from the finest legal mind to serve on the Court, but none could deny that his fundamental sense of fairness and his zeal to protect ordinary citizens from the government permeated most of his now-famous decisions.

In *Brown* the key finding does not appeal to precedent or to the history of the Fourteenth Amendment. Rather there is an emphasis on common sense, justice, and fairness that can be seen in Warren's reliance on social science and psychological research. Warren was not antigovernment, but he believed that the Constitution prohibited the government from acting unfairly against the individual. In taking this position, he carved out a powerful position for the Court as a protector of civil rights and civil liberties.

Few Supreme Court decisions impacted the country as the *Brown* decision did. The Court took five months to announce its ruling, while an expectant country waited. The delay led to rampant speculation that there was disagreement among the justices—many articles and books about the *Brown* decision say one of Warren's greatest feats early in his service as chief justice was to bring the justices into agreement on the *Brown* case. Warren, however, wrote in his memoirs some twenty years later that there was never dissension, only careful consideration:

> Contrary to speculations in the press, there had *not* been a division of opinion expressed on the Court at any time. At the weekly conference after arguments in the case, the members, conscious of its gravity and far-reaching effects, decided not to put the case to a vote until we had thoroughly explored the implications of any decision. As a result, we discussed all sides dispassionately week after week, testing arguments of counsel, suggesting various approaches, and at time acting as 'devil's advocates' in certain phases of the case, but not stating our final decision until February of 1954. At that time we voted unanimously among ourselves to declare racially segregated public schools to be unconstitutional.

Even then, though they'd reached agreement, the justices chose not to reveal their decision to the public for another three months, while Warren crafted the decision which would change the face of education in the United States. When the day came to make the announcement, on May 17, 1954, each of the justices knew it was a momentous occasion. Warren recalled the mood in the courtroom: "As we Justices marched into the courtroom on that day, there was a tenseness that I have not seen equaled before or since. When I announced that I was about to report the judgment and opinion of the Court in *Brown v. Board of Education of Topeka, Kansas*, there was a general shifting of positions in the crowded room and a rapt attention to my words."

Warren kept the opinion short, mindful that it would be published in the daily press, and he didn't want it to take up too much space. In his opinion, Warren wrote, "Segregation of white and colored children in public schools has a detrimental effect upon the colored children.

The impact is greater when it has the sanction of law, for the policy of separating the races is usually interpreted as denoting the inferiority of the negro group. A sense of inferiority affects the motivation of the child to learn."

In his memoirs, Warren recounted how those in the courtroom reacted:

> I read: "We come then to the question presented: Does segregation of children in public schools solely on the basis of race, even though the physical facilities and other tangible factors may be equal, deprive the children of the minority group of equal educational opportunities? We unanimously believe that it does." When the word "unanimously" was spoken, a wave of emotions swept the room; no words or intentional movement, yet a distinct emotional manifestation that defies description.

Warren's colleagues recognized the immense importance of what had just taken place, and its capacity to change the course of American history. They were effusive in their praise. Three of the associate justices sent handwritten notes to Warren congratulating him. The first came from Justice William O. Douglas, on May 11, six days before the decision was publicly announced. Douglas read Warren's proposed ruling and wrote to him: "I do not think I would change a single word in the memoranda you gave me this morning. The two draft opinions meet my idea exactly. You have done a beautiful job."

Two other notes came on May 17, the date of the announcement of the ruling. Justice Harold H. Burton wrote to Warren: "Today I believe has been a great day for America and the Court. Your opinions in the segregation cases were highly appropriate and were delivered in an appropriate spirit. I expect there will be no more significant decisions made during my service on the Court. I cherish the privilege of sharing in this. To you goes the credit for the character of the opinions which produced the all important unanimity. Congratulations." A final note was from Justice Felix Frankfurter, who didn't always agree with Warren's positions but enthusiastically supported his efforts to desegregate the schools. Frankfurter wrote: "This is a day that will live in glory. It is also a great day in the history of the Court, and not in the least for the course of deliberation which brought about the result. I congratulate you."

The ruling affected twenty-one states and the District of Columbia, where segregation in schools was still allowed. The effects of the ruling were not immediate; the Court gave the states some time to implement desegregation, and there were other cases that followed, in which some states and school districts argued that changing the way things were done would be a hardship. The state of Oklahoma argued that it would have to rewrite its tax laws. Florida and North Carolina argued that it went against public opinion. However, in May, 1955, the Court let the public know that the period for adjusting to the *Brown* case was over, and that school desegregation must commence "with all deliberate speed."

The impact of the *Brown* decision should be viewed in the context of the American culture at the time. Even though slavery had been abolished decades earlier, the southern states in particular had adopted a system intended to prevent the white and black races from mixing. These laws were known as "Jim Crow laws," named most likely for "Jump Jim Crow," a character in a minstrel show played by a white actor in blackface. By the mid-1800s Jim Crow had become a pejorative term for African Americans. These laws mandated the separation of blacks and whites at water fountains, lunch counters, park benches, buses, swimming pools, railroad cars, and other places.

Change did not come easily. In some places, following the mandate to end segregation, the first black students to arrive at formerly all-white schools were greeted by jeering protestors and had to be escorted by police. Warren's critics blamed him for the riots and general racial strife that followed. But despite the upheaval caused by the *Brown* decision, it seemed that once the ball began rolling in that direction, it would not be stopped. Eventually, in 1964, desegregation was formally extended to other public places such as restaurants and hotels.

A general view of the courtroom during hearings of the House Committee on Un-American Activities, led by Senator Joseph McCarthy

A NATION CHANGES

Other controversial cases followed *Brown*, among them *Watkins v. the United States*, which found in 1957 that the plaintiff was within his rights to refuse to answer questions from the House Committee on Un-American Activities, which was then scouring the country in search of suspected Communist sympathizers. This case took place while much of the nation was absorbed in a witch hunt for Communists, who were feared and reviled.

John Watkins was one of many people brought before the House Un-American Activities Committee and grilled on his political beliefs and associations. The committee was ostensibly looking for threats of "subversion" against the government. When Watkins refused to give the committee a list of names of his associates, he was convicted of failing to answer the committee's questions, which was a crime. Watkins complained that he had not been given enough time to figure out whether or not he was obligated to answer questions about his associates, which he believed to be unfairly outside the scope of the committee's authority. Warren and the rest of the Court agreed with his position, and decided that Watkins' Fifth Amendment right to due process had been violated.

Warren's opinion said that the power of Congress to conduct its own investigations was not unlimited, and that they had no authority to expose the private affairs of individuals.

In *NAACP v. Alabama*, in 1958, the Court ruled that the National Association for the Advancement of Colored People (NAACP) had the right to keep its membership list secret, in light of the state of Alabama's efforts to drive the organization out of the state. The NAACP was founded in the early 1900s, to advance racial justice for African Americans. The organization sought equality and an end to the laws that mandated segregation in schools, housing, transportation, and public places. In the 1950s, this was considered a radical idea, and some thought the NAACP to be full of radicals. Even though the *Brown v. Board of Education* case had been decided four years earlier, some southern states were still resisting the move toward desegregation.

Authorities in the state of Alabama falsely blamed the NAACP for instigating the Montgomery Bus Boycott in 1955, which followed the famous arrest of African American seamstress Rosa Parks, who refused to sit in the back of a bus or give up her seat to a white person, as required by law. The NAACP had been operating in Alabama since 1918, but in 1956 the state of Alabama demanded a copy of the NAACP's membership list, charging that the group had violated a state business law requiring corporations to register with the state before transacting business. The group didn't want to divulge the names, in order to protect its members, because the civil rights movement was underway and African Americans in the South were often subjected to harassment and violence. For its refusal to divulge the list, the NAACP was found in contempt of court and fined $100,000—a huge sum of money in those years.

The NAACP appealed to the Supreme Court, arguing that the Fourteenth Amendment guarantees rights to freedom of speech and assembly. Ruling in the NAACP's favor, the court wrote that revealing the group's membership list would be likely to affect adversely the ability of the group and its members to pursue their efforts to foster beliefs which they admittedly have the right to advocate. The Court also noted that if the membership was revealed, people might withdraw from the group and others be dissuaded from joining, out of fear of the consequences.

Warren continued with his drive toward racial equality with the

Loving v. Virginia case in 1967, which overturned the convictions and prison sentences of Richard Loving, a white man, and his wife, Mildred Jeter, a black woman. The couple married in Washington, D.C., then returned to their home state of Virginia, in which marriage between the races was forbidden. The state's lawyers argued that God did not intend for the races to mix, but the Warren Court disagreed, finding that the Virginia law against interracial marriage had no valid purpose other than to enforce racial discrimination.

The Warren court didn't just tackle racial prejudice. It also took on religion, specifically the then-common practice of having prayer in schools. In *Engel v. Vitale* in 1962, the Court found that schools may not force children to pray in school. The prayer in question was short: "Almighty God, we acknowledge our dependence upon Thee, and we beg Thy blessings upon us, our parents, our teachers and our Country." The board of regents of the state of New York's public education system wrote this prayer in 1951. While they acknowledged that formal religion did not belong in public schools, they also recommended the prayer to local school boards, reasoning that teaching children that God is their creator would provide them additional security.

Some school boards adopted it, including the one in New Hyde Park, New York, which voted in 1958 to begin each school day with the prayer. Some parents objected, including Steven I. Engel who, along with four other parents, asked the state court to order the prayers stopped. The lawsuit was filed against William J. Vitale Jr., one of the school board members, and the rest of the board. In court, the lawyers for the school board argued that prayer provided moral training for good citizenship. They said any child could be excused from praying, upon request. The New York state courts approved that position, saying that by adopting the prayer the courts were not preferring or teaching religion, as long as students were not compelled to pray against their will.

The Warren Court accepted the case for review, and in 1962 concluded that since the constitution guarantees freedom of religious expression, no governmental entity could compose official prayers for Americans to recite.

In another case, *Griswold v. Connecticut*, the Warren Court established that there is a constitutional right to privacy. The controversial ruling struck down a Connecticut law enacted in 1879 that prohibited anyone from using contraception or even disseminating information about birth control. Estelle T. Griswold was the executive director of the Planned Parenthood League of Connecticut. She opened a birth control clinic which gave information, instruction, and other medical advice to married couples about birth control. She and a colleague were arrested, convicted, and fined one hundred dollars each.

Griswold's attorneys argued that the constitution guarantees a right to privacy for married couples in such matters, and the Court agreed. Although there is no specific guarantee to privacy in the Constitution, the justices found that in this case the Fourteenth Amendment had been violated. The Fourteenth Amendment says that no state shall make or enforce any law which deprives any person of life, liberty, or property, without due process of law, nor deny any person the equal protection of the laws.

Throughout his term as chief justice, Warren made it clear he favored individual liberties and freedom of speech, which he felt overwhelmingly outweighed government restrictions. Whether Warren and his fellow justices were merely following along with changing times, or leading the way in creating the changes that altered the nation is up for debate. Some saw Warren's unabashed liberalism as a betrayal, because they expected him to be a conservative jurist. But Warren insisted he had not changed. "People do misinterpret a public figure's instincts and motivations, and I have often encountered this in my career," Warren wrote in his memoirs.

> It has been written that there was nothing in my background to presage my so-called 'liberal' decisions on the Supreme Court. This notion has always been something of a mystery to me. Of course, I could well have some prejudice, as most of us do, in favor of my own consistency, but my actions have been exposed to the public constantly for more than half a century, and I feel that my views and actions in later years are but an outgrowth of the earlier ones.

Despite that statement, just before his death Warren was interviewed for an article in the *New York Times* newspaper, in which he conceded:

save our republic

IMPEACH
EARL WARREN

CONT/   JUDICIAL   REEDUCATION. P. O. BOX 541. SAN GABRIEL

Senator John H. Rousselot standing beneath a billboard calling for Warren's impeachment

"I do not see how a man could be on the Court and not change his views substantially over a period of years."

Nevertheless, Warren had become so hated in some sectors that Old West-style "Wanted" posters began cropping up around the country, calling for Warren's impeachment for, among other things, being a "dangerous and subversive character." The first known call for Warren's impeachment was taped to a bulletin board in a post office in San Francisco at Seventh and Mission streets, and was reported to the FBI on October 14, 1958.

The poster, which featured a "mug shot" of Warren's face and profile, said Warren was "an apparent sympathiser of the Communist Party" and a "rabid agitator for compulsory racial mongrelization." The flier also said Warren had "illegally transformed the Supreme Court into a Soviet-style politburo"—a serious charge during an era when fear of Russians and Communism was rampant throughout the country. Ironically, the poster also cautioned that "Earl Warren is a fanatic who will stop at nothing to achieve his goals." Warren later said the signs didn't really bother him at all. "I never took any great offense at it; in fact, I could smile at it, but it took me a little time to get my wife accustomed to smiling at those signs."

Warren, taking a break from his judicial duties, reads a newspaper in Capitol Park.

YOU HAVE THE RIGHT
TO REMAIN SILENT

Undeterred by the critics, Warren and his fellow justices continued with a series of rulings that preserved the constitutional rights of the accused. In *Mapp v. Ohio*, the Court overturned the conviction of a woman who was convicted of possession of obscene materials. In May 1957 the police came to Dolree Mapp's home in search of a suspected bomber. She wouldn't let them in without a warrant. Finally, about an hour later they forced their way in and held up a piece of paper when she demanded to see their search warrant. The police handcuffed her for being "belligerent," and searched her home. They didn't find the suspect but did find books determined to be obscene, in a trunk.

Mapp said she had no knowledge of what was in the trunk, which she said was left behind by a former boarder. Yet she was taken to trial on a charge of possessing pornography and convicted. The officers and the prosecutor never did show Mapp or her attorney the search warrant they supposedly had, nor did they ever explain why they refused to show it.

The Fourth Amendment specifically requires officers to have detailed warrants for searches and arrests, and the states had similar laws.

But those laws were routinely ignored for years. In a 1914 Supreme Court case, the Court ruled that if federal officers seized property illegally, it could not be admitted in federal court. But the states were left to do as they pleased, until the *Mapp* case ruling of 1961. Ohio's attorneys argued that since the objectionable material was taken from a trunk—an inanimate object—and not taken forcibly from Dolree Mapp in person, that it was okay because she hadn't suffered an illegal seizure of her possessions. But in the *Mapp* case, for the first time, the Supreme Court ruled that evidence obtained during a search that violates the Fourth Amendment protection against illegal search and seizure should not be admissible in state courts.

The *Gault* case in 1967 involved a fifteen-year-old boy accused of making an obscene phone call to a neighbor, which he denied. His parents weren't notified of his arrest, however, because they were at work, and he was interrogated without a lawyer present. The boy was convicted without ever having the chance to face his accuser. The Court found that juveniles accused of crimes have the same constitutional due process rights as adults—including, in this case, the right to timely notification of the charges, the right to confront witnesses, the right against self-incrimination and the right to counsel.

Despite his rulings in favor of a woman accused of possession of obscene materials, and a boy accused of making an obscene phone call, Warren was personally against pornography of any kind. Even though he strongly believed it was the right thing to do to uphold the constitutional rights of the accused, he reportedly once told a man he had just met on an airplane that if a "smut peddler" were to sell pornography to his daughters, Warren would throttle him with his bare hands.

Warren did have his limits as a judge when it came to this topic. In 1964 the Court majority ruled that erotic materials could not be suppressed by government officials unless the material was considered objectionable under a national standard. Warren dissented on that case, writing that he believed each community should be free to ban material that violates the values of that community.

Nevertheless, most of Warren's rulings favored the rights of the accused, regardless of the criminal charge. The Court began to earn a reputation for being "anti-police," primarily for decisions that upheld the rights of the poor and those at the margins of society, who were most susceptible to being abused by police and other authorities.

Gideon v. Wainwright, in 1963, was the case that determined that all people accused of crimes have the right to an attorney, even if they can't afford one. Clarence Earl Gideon was accused of breaking into the Bay Harbor pool hall in Panama City, Florida. After the burglary, Gideon was found nearby with a bottle of wine and some change in his pockets, and was arrested. He tried to get a court-appointed lawyer but failed, because at the time the state of Florida only afforded public lawyers to those facing the death penalty. He went to trial but didn't do a very good job of defending himself, and was convicted of breaking and entering and petty larceny.

But Gideon then did something unusual. In a handwritten petition to the U.S. Supreme Court, he asked it to review his case. He started studying law while in prison and concluded that his constitutional rights were violated. The language he used in his letter was formal and appropriate for Court: "Comes now the petitioner, Clarence Earl Gideon, a citizen of the United States of America, in proper person and appearing as his own counsel." Gideon argued that a man with no legal training shouldn't be expected to represent himself at trial just because he is too poor to hire an attorney.

The state of Florida's lawyers argued that this was a matter best left to the states to decide individually. However, the Supreme Court found that the Sixth Amendment guarantees the right to a fair trial, which includes the right to have an attorney's representation, since no person without a law degree could reasonably be expected to understand all the nuances of the law. Gideon won a new trial, with a court-appointed lawyer, and was acquitted.

A few months later, in a speech to the New England Law Institute, U.S. Attorney General Robert F. Kennedy said:

> If an obscure Florida convict named Clarence Earl Gideon had not sat down in prison with a pencil and paper to write a letter to the Supreme Court, and if the Supreme Court had not taken the trouble to look for merit in that one crude petition among all the bundles of mail it must receive every day, the vast machinery of American law would have gone on functioning undisturbed. But Gideon did write that letter, the Court did look into his case, and he was retried with the help of a competent defense counsel, found not guilty, and released from prison after two years of punishment for a crime he did not commit, and the whole course of American legal history has been changed.

Perhaps the most famous, or infamous, of the Warren Court's rulings benefiting accused criminals was the *Miranda v. Arizona* case in 1966. This was the decision that led to the nationwide rule that the accused must be read their rights, or "Mirandized," as it has come to be known. Even those who have never been arrested are now familiar with this rule, as nearly every subsequent movie and television show about criminal justice includes, at some point, the now well-worn phrase: "You have the right to remain silent. If you give up that right, anything you say can and will be used against you in a court of law . . . "

Ernesto Miranda, accused of rape, kidnapping, and robbery, was not a particularly sympathetic character. This case, more than any other, earned Warren a reputation among his critics for "coddling" criminals. The police in Phoenix, Arizona, suspected Miranda of being a serial rapist, who had kidnapped, raped, and robbed several young women. In 1963 the license plate on his truck was recognized by the brother of a rape victim, and Miranda was apprehended.

After two hours of interrogation, Miranda confessed. He was taken to a lineup and, upon seeing the victim, blurted out, "That's the girl." He then wrote down his confession, writing at the top of each sheet, as instructed by police, that his confession had been made voluntarily and with full knowledge of his legal rights. However, that wasn't true, since he was never informed of his rights to remain silent or to have an attorney present during questioning. At trial, Miranda was convicted of rape and kidnapping and sentenced to twenty to thirty years in prison. After the Arizona Supreme Court upheld his conviction on appeal, Miranda's case was taken up by the American Civil Liberties Union, which found him a lawyer free of charge and took the case to the U.S. Supreme Court. The Court found that Miranda's Fifth Amendment right against self-incrimination, and his Sixth Amendment right to have a lawyer were violated.

While the *Miranda* case was a huge new development in the rights of the accused, things didn't change much for Miranda himself. Miranda won a new trial, and even though his confession was not admitted as evidence the second time, he was again convicted of kidnapping and rape. He was released from prison in 1972, but went back to prison a few times on various charges. When not incarcerated, he found an odd sort of fame by carrying around the cards police were required to have with the Miranda warning printed on them, so officers could remember to advise arrestees of their rights. Miranda autographed the warning cards for $1.50 apiece. In 1976 he was stabbed to death in a dispute over a three dollar bet during a poker game. The suspect was duly advised of his Miranda rights, chose not to speak to investigators, and was released pending further investigation. He then disappeared, and the case was never resolved.

Despite his success in protecting the rights of the accused, Warren always claimed that the cases involving voters' rights were the most important.

Warren served three terms as the governor of California, and believed in the principle of "one person, one vote."

ONE MAN, ONE VOTE

A series of cases came before the Court involving apportion- ment, or the way the population of a legislative district is counted to ensure equal representation by the elected of- ficials. Each of these cases gave Warren the opportunity to enforce his oft-stated belief in "one person, one vote," or the premise that everyone should have an equal say in how their governmental representatives are chosen.

The problem of congressional districts having not been redrawn in years was pervasive throughout many states by the 1950s. In the year 1950, in Vermont, one elected representative had forty-nine people in his district, while another district had 33,155 people. That same year, in Connecticut, the districts were so skewed that 9 percent of the people could technically have elected more than half the state's representatives. By 1955, the Colorado legislature was giving the city of Denver $2.3 million a year for its schools, which educated 90,000 children, while a semirural county in the state received more, $2.4 million, to educate 18,000 students.

The U.S. Supreme Court had the opportunity once before to rectify some of these inequities in a case on apportionment that came before it in 1946. But the Court had ruled that it was a political matter for the states, and none of the Court's business. That all changed during the Warren years.

One of the most famous of these cases was *Baker v. Carr*, in 1962. Charles W. Baker of Memphis, Tennessee, and nine other voters, sued Joe C. Carr, secretary of state of Tennessee, to change the state's election procedures. Carr didn't draw the lines of the legislative districts, but in his position he was ultimately responsible for the actions of the state legislature, which did.

The Tennessee constitution held that electoral districts should be changed every ten years. But at that point it hadn't been done in more than sixty years, since 1901. Because so many people moved from farms into cities during the first half of the twentieth century, that meant people still living in the rural areas held a disproportionate amount of power on Election Day.

The lawyers representing the state of Tennessee didn't argue that what had happened was right; they argued that the question of how to handle state legislative districts is properly left up to the states to decide. The Warren Court disagreed, choosing to insert the Court into questions of states' rights in order to protect the people. In this case the Court ruled that if a state lets one person's vote count for more than another's because they are in different districts, then the state is denying its citizens their constitutional rights to equal protection under the law. The Court also decided that it was proper for the judiciary to get involved in this issue, rather than leaving it up to the states.

More than two dozen similar cases followed, which reshaped voters' rights in America. One of those cases was *Reynolds v. Sims*, in 1964. While the *Carr* case established that redistricting was not purely a political question that was best left up to the individual states to decide, Reynolds took it a step further and required state legislative districts to be roughly equal in population. Before this case was decided, urban areas were often badly underrepresented.

In *Reynolds*, voters in Jefferson County, Alabama, challenged the apportionment of the legislature. This was the first case in which the principal "one person, one vote" was applied. Writing for the majority opinion, Warren wrote:

> Legislators represent people, not trees or acres. Legislators are elected by voters, not farms or cities or economic interests . . . Representative government is, in essence, self-government through the medium of elected representatives of the people, and each and every citizen has an inalienable right to full and effective participation in the political processes of his State's legislative bodies. Most citizens can achieve this participation only as qualified voters through the election of legislators to represent them. Full and effective participation by all citizens in state government requires, therefore, that each citizen have an equally effective voice in the election of members of his state legislature. Modern and viable state government needs, and the Constitution demands, no less.

While Warren appeared bent on interpreting the Constitution to fit his view of how things should be, his actions were not without critics even within the court. In the *Reynolds* case, conservative Justice John M. Harlan dissented, and leveled a criticism that seemed to be about more than just that case; perhaps it was meant as a general lecture directed at Warren, who seemed more and more determined to exact his brand of social justice. In his dissent, Harlan wrote:

> These decisions give support to a current mistaken view of the Constitution and the constitutional function of this Court. This view, in a nutshell, is that every major social ill in this country can find its cure in some constitutional "principle," and that this Court should "take the lead" in promoting reform when other branches of Government fail to act. The Constitution is not a panacea for every blot upon the public welfare, nor should this Court, ordained as a judicial body, be thought of as a general haven for reform movements.

While the right-wingers assailed Warren for his left-leaning rulings which tended to favor the poor, accused criminals, and non-whites, the criticism levied by Harlan was often echoed in legal circles: that Warren tended to shape rulings more with regard to his ethics, than to the law. Warren himself readily admitted that his own experiences and emotions played a part. In an interview two years after his retirement, Warren said:

> Every man's judgment is colored by his experiences in life and the way he reacts to those experiences . . . Every man is a creature of the conditions that he has faced in life and the interpretations he puts upon those things, it seems to me. And all those things go into the formation of opinions. I don't see how you can help it. I've heard some judges who say that they just put the law here and the Constitution here and if the law conforms to the Constitution as they read it there, it's good, and if it doesn't it's bad. That's a lot of malarkey . . . It just can't be that simple in 999 out of 1,000 cases.

Nevertheless, it is undisputed that the Warren Court and the chief justice's overriding sense of fairness set off a series of changes in the country. In addition to these well-known rulings, in its sixteen years the Warren Court also put a curb on government wiretapping, extended the boundaries of free speech, restored freedom of foreign travel, ruled that federal prisoners could sue the government for injuries sustained in jail, and said wages could not be garnished (taken out of someone's paycheck) without a hearing.

Responding to critics who maintained the Supreme Court should not be in the business of changing society, Warren said, "Almost every important decision of the Supreme Court changes some social condition in the country, and the Court shouldn't run away from its jurisdiction just because it affects a social condition." Likewise, Warren never shied away from taking on controversial cases, as past Supreme Court justices had. "I think in the past it has been done many times, and I think that where that has been done it's similar to sweeping dust under the rug and leaving it for a future generation. And we're paying the price right now."

A *New York Times* obituary, published after Warren's death in 1974, summarized his legacy on the court well: "Mr. Warren's Court, amid much dispute, elaborated a doctrine of fairness in such areas as criminal justice, voting rights, legislative districting, employment, housing, transportation and education. In so doing, the Chief Justice of the United States contributed greatly to a reshaping of the country's social and political institutions."

The presidential motorcade in Dallas, Texas, on November 22, 1963, the day John F. Kennedy was assassinated

THE WARREN COMMISSION

On November 22, 1963, a tragedy shook the nation: John F. Kennedy Jr., the popular young president, was shot to death while riding in an open convertible in a motorcade through Dallas, Texas. Kennedy was handsome and charismatic, and his wife Jackie was beautiful and considered one of the most fashionable women of her time.

Kennedy was a Democrat, and the public had high hopes for his leadership as the country moved through a turbulent time. Kennedy was elected in 1960 and was facing reelection the next year. It was hoped the motorcade would cement his popularity in a city that didn't support his presidency during the last election. On that day Kennedy and his wife were riding atop the rear hood of a car, waving to the adoring crowd when it happened, at about half past noon. Shots rang out, and Kennedy slumped into his wife's lap, mortally wounded. Texas governor John Connally, who was also riding in the car, was wounded. The assassination of the president occurred in view of hundreds of shocked onlookers.

Within a few hours, police arrested a suspect: a loner named Lee Harvey Oswald, an employee of the Texas School Book Depository, who disliked the United States and longed to live in the Soviet Union. Based on what witnesses told them, police determined Oswald shot the president from a sixth-floor window inside the Depository, and they found empty cartridge cases and an Italian bolt-action rifle on that floor. While police were questioning employees who were working there that day, the building superintendent noticed that one of the employees was missing: Oswald. Within an hour of the assassination, Oswald shot and killed a policeman, before he was cornered inside a movie theater.

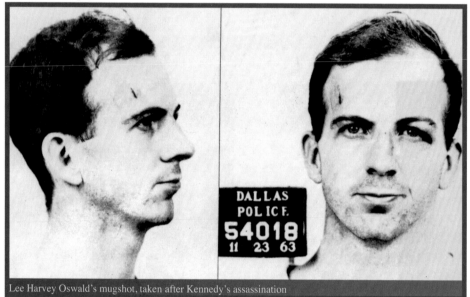
Lee Harvey Oswald's mugshot, taken after Kennedy's assassination

Police didn't have much opportunity to interrogate Oswald about his motives, and during what little interrogation time they had, Oswald steadfastly denied shooting the president. Two days later, as Oswald was taken by authorities to be transferred from the city jail to the county jail, a man stepped out of the crowd and shot Oswald to death with a handgun at close range, right in front of the police and the press, while the television cameras rolled. The shooter was Jack Ruby, a Dallas nightclub operator. Ruby told police he killed Oswald "in a temporary fit of depression and rage over the President's death." Thus began a decades-long dispute over whether Kennedy's murder was merely the act of a lone angry man, or whether the two men were embroiled in some kind of top-secret conspiracy.

The day it happened, the justices were in conference and received a note that the president had been shot, so they adjourned immediately. That evening Warren met the newly sworn-in president, Lyndon Baines Johnson, at the airport at Andrews Air Force Base in Maryland, as he arrived back from Dallas, and offered his condolences. Although the chief justice traditionally administers the oath of office to the president, Johnson, who was Kennedy's vice president, had already been sworn in by a federal district court judge on the airplane, because of the emergency circumstances.

One week after Kennedy's death, Johnson called on Warren to serve as the head of a special committee to investigate the assassination. Warren was very reluctant to do so, because he felt working on special committees conflicted with his duties on the Supreme Court. Warren later said, "Practically all of us had expressed the belief that it was not wise for members of the Supreme Court to accept positions on presidential commissions. I had personally expressed that view and I still think as a general thing it's a sound rule . . . We have enough work to do here." Johnson sent the solicitor general and the deputy attorney general to ask Warren to serve on the commission, but Warren told them he didn't think he should. Warren thought that was the end of it.

Then, about an hour later, Warren received a call from the White House and was informed that the president wanted to see him right away. Johnson pressured Warren, citing national defense and a growing sense of worry among the public that Kennedy's assassination may have been orchestrated by the Communist countries of Russia and Cuba. Johnson even raised the specter of a possible nuclear war that would annihilate millions of American citizens if Warren didn't agree to take the post. "The President told me that he was greatly disturbed by the rumors that were going around the world about a conspiracy and so forth, and that he thought that it might—because it involved both (Soviet Union leader Nikita) Khrushchev and (Cuban Prime Minister Fidel) Castro—that it might even catapult us into a nuclear war if it got a head start, you know, and kept growing."

Johnson then upped the ante, telling Warren he'd discussed the matter with Robert McNamara, the secretary of defense. "McNamara had told him that if we got into a nuclear war that at the first strike we would lose sixty million people. And he impressed upon me the great danger that was involved in having something develop from all of this talk." Johnson went on to flatter Warren, in his continued attempts to persuade him to lead the commission, by telling him, "This thing is of such great importance that the world is entitled to have the thing presided over by the highest judicial officer of the United States."

"You've worn a uniform, you were in the Army in World War I," Johnson said to Warren. "This job is more important than anything you ever did in the uniform." So Warren finally agreed, becoming the head of the President's Commission on the Assassination of President Kennedy, which eventually came to be known, simply, as the "Warren Commission."

The ten months he worked on the commission were "the unhappiest time of my life," Warren later told a *New York Times* reporter. "To review the terrible happenings of that assassination every day (was) a traumatic experience." He worked on the commission almost every day until midnight, after his duties at the Court were finished for the day.

"The only reason I undertook the commission was the gravity of the situation . . . There was no way of holding a trial, for Oswald was dead and the country needed to have the facts of the killing brought out. But it isn't a good thing for a Justice to undertake such duties."

Warren maintained that the investigation was as thorough as possible, leaving no stone unturned. Warren insisted even years later that there was never any evidence uncovered to show that the conclusions of the commission were wrong. The 888-page report was presented to the president on September, 24, 1964. It begins:

> The assassination of John Fitzgerald Kennedy on November 22, 1963, was a cruel and shocking act of violence directed against a man, a family, a nation, and against all mankind. A young and vigorous leader whose years of public and private life stretched before him was the victim of the fourth Presidential assassination in the history of a country dedicated to the concepts of reasoned argument and peaceful political change.

The authors, mindful of their role in history, added that the commission was created "in recognition of the right of people everywhere to full and truthful knowledge concerning these events. This report endeavors to fulfill that right and to appraise this tragedy by the light of reason and the standard of fairness."

The report painted a picture of Oswald as a lonely, angry man, whose psychiatric problems started at a young age. He was always in trouble with his teachers because of his behavior. Oswald's mother married and divorced three times and moved her sons around the country often. He dropped out of school at age sixteen, and about that time started reading Communist literature and declared himself to be a Marxist.

Oswald joined the U.S. Marine Corps, where he earned "marksman" status as a sharpshooter. But while he was still in the Marines Oswald started telling people he wanted to go to Cuba and join the Cuban army. After being discharged from the military in 1959, Oswald flew to France, ostensibly to go to college in Switzerland, but soon caught a train to Moscow and applied for citizenship in the Soviet Union. But his application was rejected six days later and Oswald was ordered to leave the Soviet Union. The night he learned of his impending deportation, Oswald slashed his wrist in an apparent suicide attempt at his hotel. He was hospitalized, and upon his release he went to the U.S. Embassy in Moscow and asked to renounce his United States citizenship. He handed the embassy officials a note, which stated: "I am a Marxist." He never was granted Soviet citizenship, but he was allowed to stay for a couple years, during which time Oswald met and married a Russian woman named Marina.

In 1962 the couple returned to the U.S. and moved to Texas. Living in Dallas, Oswald "showed disdain for democracy, capitalism, and American society in general," according to the Warren Commission report. Oswald had a couple brushes with the law; he tried to shoot and kill a retired U.S. Army major general in April of 1963, and a few months later was arrested during a scuffle that occurred while he was distributing pro-Castro leaflets. He lost two jobs that year, and took a bus to Mexico City in late September, where he tried to gain permission to travel to Cuba. His efforts to obtain a visa to Cuba were denied, so he returned to Dallas, arriving October 3. He took the job at the School Book Depository on October 16, less than a month before the Kennedy murder. When Oswald left the house on the day of the assassination, he left behind his wedding ring and his wallet, which was full of cash.

The Texas School Book Depository in Dallas, Texas. Lee Harvey Oswald allegedly shot John F. Kennedy from the sixth floor (the square window on the right).

The report concluded that Oswald, firing from the sixth floor of the book depository, fired three shots. The report also stated there was "very persuasive evidence from the experts to indicate that the same bullet which pierced the president's throat also caused Governor Connally's wounds." This part of the report was widely mocked as the "magic bullet theory," since many found it unlikely that a single bullet traveling in a straight line could enter the back of the president's neck, exit through the front of his throat and nick his necktie, then continue on to hit Connally below the right armpit, exiting through his chest and then passing through Connally's right wrist and wounding his thigh.

Furthermore, the report found no evidence that either Oswald or Ruby were involved in any conspiracy, domestic or foreign, to assassinate Kennedy. They found no evidence Oswald was assisted by anyone in planning the shooting, or that he was involved in any conspiracy with Communists, despite his travel to the Soviet Union and the attempted trip to Cuba. The report stated: "Because of the difficulty of proving negatives to a certainty the possibility of others being involved with either Oswald or Ruby cannot be established categorically, but if there is any such evidence it has been beyond the reach of all the investigative agencies and resources of the United States and has not come to the attention of this Commission."

The report also blames the police and press for error-filled reports that were made public in the confusion of the initial hours and days after the shooting, contributing to the notion that something was amiss with the investigation. "The numerous statements, sometimes erroneous, made to the press by various local law enforcement officials, during this time of confusion and disorder in the police station . . . helped to create doubts, speculations, and fears in the mind of the public which might otherwise not have arisen."

The report was made public three days after it was delivered to Johnson, and two months later the commission published twenty-six volumes of supporting documents, which included transcripts of the testimony of 552 people. There were also more than 3,100 exhibits. All of the materials are at the U.S. National Archives and Records Administration in Maryland.

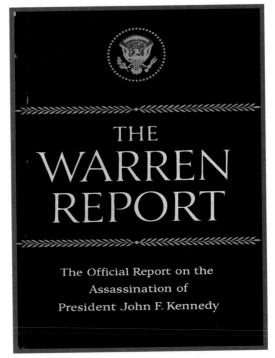

THE
WARREN
REPORT

The Official Report on the
Assassination of
President John F. Kennedy

The report remains highly controversial. Then, as now, many people refused to believe that Kennedy's killing was the work of a single gunman. Also, some critics believe there was a cover-up involved; the original FBI report on Kennedy's autopsy describes another bullet wound in the president's back, which isn't mentioned in the Warren Commission report.

No one seems to know the location of the photos taken of the autopsy, which were not presented to the commission. They might have been turned over to the Kennedy family, or given to the Secret Service, or just destroyed by the passage of time. At least one article, printed in *Esquire* magazine in 1966, blames the commission itself for the rise of the conspiracy theories. "While the Commission was obviously intent on proving there was no conspiracy, selecting testimony and evidence for their Report that particularly suited them, the assassination buffs have responded by being suspicious of everything in which the Commission put credence."

Many thought that the Warren Commission hearings were conducted in secret, which is not quite accurate. The hearings were closed to the public, unless the witness who was testifying asked for an open hearing. Only one did. None of the witnesses were prohibited from talking about their testimony after they were done, and their testimony was subsequently made public. Some of the records remained sealed for a time, however, for a period that was supposed to be seventy-five years, in order to protect innocent people who might be damaged by their relationship with participants in the case. However, that rule was repealed and now all the Warren Commission's records are public except those containing information about people's personal tax returns. Those final records are scheduled to be made public in 2017.

Even the release of the public records has not quelled the conspiracy theories. Many people believed then, and still do, that Oswald was involved in a conspiracy to kill the president, perhaps orchestrated by the U.S. government, the CIA in particular, or, as others have speculated, it was a killing ordered by the Mafia. Some thought that Oswald's affection for Communism pointed to a left-wing conspiracy. Others thought that right-wingers wanted the liberal Democrat Kennedy gone. Even President Johnson once commented, in his pre-interview remarks prior to going on the air for a CBS television interview with Walter Cronkite, that he "had never been satisfied that it wasn't a foreign conspiracy." His remarks, however, garnered little notice because there was a provision in the president's contract with CBS that he could have any comments deleted that involved internal security.

But, according to Warren, there was no evidence to support any of the popular conspiracy theories. There was one witness they heard testimony from, a man named Mark Lane, who insisted the assassination was the work of some influential men in the Texas oil industry who wanted the liberal Democrat president dead. Lane was a lawyer and a friend of Kennedy's. The man insisted repeatedly that he knew of witnesses, but said their names were confidential and he could not divulge them. According to Warren, Lane never did come up with the name of any witness who could prove his theory, which didn't stop him from giving a series of lectures in Europe promoting his "big oil" conspiracy views. Lane later wrote a book detailing his beliefs in a conspiracy, called *Plausible Denial*, which is still popular with JFK assassination conspiracy buffs decades afterward.

Doubting the Warren report's conclusions became a popular, even obsessive, pastime for many Americans. An article published in *Esquire* magazine three years after the report's release summed it up:

> The Warren Commission was supposed to end all doubts about the assassination of President John F. Kennedy. Tragically, it hasn't. The distinguished members of the Commission never intended that their Report should become the basis for an amateur detective game. Yet this is precisely what is happening. A growing number of people are spending their leisure hours scouring the Commission's Report and the twenty-six volumes of testimony and exhibits for possible clues to a conspiracy. Others, using high-powered magnifying glasses and infrared lights, are scrutinizing photographs of the assassination scene, hoping to find snipers concealed in the shrubbery.

The *Esquire* article continued: "This phenomenon would not be particularly disturbing if the players were merely kooks. However, most of them are not. Assassination buffs apparently are serious people . . . bent on solving what they consider to be an unsolved mystery. Perhaps this is all part of the American folklore tradition of amateurs stepping in and solving cases that baffle the police."

Several of the prevailing theories had Oswald's killer, Jack Ruby, involved in the conspiracy, and many believed Ruby was sent to dispatch Oswald before he could talk about it. During the investigation, Warren personally took testimony from Ruby, who wouldn't talk to anyone on the commission but the chief justice. Warren said Ruby wanted to have the FBI give him a lie detector test, so people would know he was telling the truth, that he had nothing to do with Oswald or any assassination conspiracy.

The FBI did, in fact, administer the test, and Ruby passed it, according to Warren. They did not, however, bring Ruby from his prison cell in Dallas to Washington, D.C., for the testimony as he wished, since Warren was concerned about security. So Warren went to Dallas to meet with Oswald's killer.

> I was satisfied myself that he didn't know and never did know Oswald, never heard of him. But the fellow was clearly delusional when I talked to him he took me aside and he said, 'Hear those voices, hear those voices?' He thought they were Jewish children and Jewish women who were being put to death in the building there . . . Oh, the poor fellow, I really felt sorry for him.

Warren speculated that the readiness of people to believe in the conspiracy theories may have come from stories of conspiracies throughout European and South American history, replete with palace guard defections and peasant uprisings. In the U.S., however, assassinations of leaders have mostly been committed by "demented people," Warren said. Even years later, Warren still stood his ground when asked about the report. In 1971 he said, "I occasionally see (other commission members) and I ask them if they have ever heard of anything to discredit the report factually, and they say no, they've never heard of anything. And I think that's true."

Three subsequent investigations by the U.S. government agreed with the Warren Commission's conclusion that Kennedy was hit from behind by two bullets. One was a panel convened by Attorney General Ramsey Clark in 1968. That didn't deter Warren's old nemesis, Richard M. Nixon, from joining in the chorus of skeptics. While Nixon was campaigning for president in 1968, he was publicly critical of the Warren report, and accused Warren of favoring criminal forces. After Nixon was elected, Chief Justice Warren was obligated—however awkward the circumstances—to administer the oath of office to the new president. Since so many people were still unsatisfied, two more government investigations followed: the Rockefeller Commission investigation in 1975, which agreed with the Warren report, and the House Select Committee on Assassinations, which reexamined the forensic evidence in 1978 and 1979. The House Select Committee upheld the Warren Commission's conclusion that Kennedy was killed by Oswald, who was firing from the sixth floor of the Book Depository building, but also concluded that Oswald probably acted as part of a conspiracy.

The committee's finding was based in part on some controversial acoustic evidence, consisting of tape recordings made at the time of the shooting. In the tapes, it sounds like there was a second gunman, firing shots from a so-called "grassy knoll," which was part of the landscaped Dealey Plaza, on a level with the president's car. The House committee concluded that there were four gunshots, and that Oswald had fired the first, second and fourth, but a second person had fired the third shot from behind a picket fence on the grass as the president's car drove by. They concluded that one shot had missed, however, and it was Oswald's bullets that killed the president and wounded Connally. The House commission also concluded that the Warren Commission was reasonably thorough and acted in good faith but had failed to adequately consider the possibility of a conspiracy.

John F. Kennedy Jr. was not the last Kennedy to be assassinated. On June 5, 1968, his brother Robert, a U.S. senator, was also killed. Robert F. Kennedy was the Democratic nominee for president, and with him gone, Warren feared there was nothing to stop his enemy Richard Nixon, the Republican nominee, from winning the presidential election. Warren announced his desire to retire days later.

Lyndon B. Johnson (left) is sworn in as president of the United States by Chief Justice Earl Warren (right) as Lady Bird Johnson and Hubert Humphrey (center) look on.

FINAL YEARS

Warren retired from the Supreme Court on June 23, 1969. It was a process some regarded with suspicion, as Warren originally let President Johnson know, in a written memo on June 13, 1968, that he wished to retire "at your pleasure" due to his advanced age. Warren was seventy-seven years old. Johnson responded that he would accept Warren's retirement as soon as a qualified candidate was found.

Johnson by this time was a "lame duck" president in his last term of office. Some believed this was a pre-emptive move by Warren to keep Nixon, a conservative Republican, from naming his successor. Warren thought, correctly, that Nixon would win the presidential election later that year. U.S. Senator Sam Ervin questioned whether Warren planned to retire if a liberal justice was not named as his replacement. Warren maintained that he did not try to influence whom Johnson chose as his successor. Years afterward, Warren said, "President Johnson, when I gave him my notification of retirement, asked me if I had any candidates, and I said, 'No, Mr. President, that's your problem.'"

Johnson nominated Associate Justice Abe Fortas, whom Warren liked because his liberal views were in line with Warren's own.

However, during the confirmation process, Republicans and conservative Democrats managed to block the Senate from taking action on the nomination. Fortas, fearing his nomination would not be confirmed, withdrew his name from consideration. Later, it was revealed that Fortas had improperly accepted a $20,000 fee from a foundation. Even though he returned the money, Fortas was forced to resign from the Supreme Court under a cloud of suspicion.

Warren decided he would stay on until the end of the court's term that year, in June. Nixon was elected Johnson's successor, and it appeared at that point there would be no way to avoid having the next chief justice appointed by the new president.

Nixon nominated Warren E. Berger as Warren's replacement, even though Warren didn't think Berger was worthy. Just a week before he stepped down, Warren led the Court in another important ruling, in which the justices decided that the House of Representatives could not deny a seat in the House to a representative who was duly elected by his constituents. The man in question was Adam Clayton Powell Jr., an African American from Harlem in New York, who annoyed some with his flamboyance. Powell was first elected in 1944, but came under fire for allegations that he misappropriated funds from the Education and Labor Committee, of which he was chairman, for his own personal use, including vacations to the Bahamas.

In 1967 the members of the House voted to exclude him, but he was so popular among his constituents that he won the special election called to fill the vacancy created by his absence. He had retaken his seat in the House by the time the ruling was handed down in 1969, but at least Warren was satisfied that the Court had made it clear that voters could not be denied the right to elect their own representatives. (In 1970, a year after the ruling, Powell was defeated during a reelection bid, and moved to the island of Bimini in the Bahamas.)

On Warren's last day on the bench, June 23, 1969, the justices handed down three decisions. As befitted Warren's controversial history on the Court, all three were regarding criminal cases, and all the decisions broke new legal ground in protecting the rights of the accused.

Warren then retired. He remarked at the time, "I would like the Court to be remembered as the people's court," underscoring his commitment to the rights of individuals. Though he had at times expressed a desire to return to California after his retirement, Warren and his wife continued to live in

Washington, D.C., and Warren kept a small office at the Supreme Court building. He busied himself writing his memoirs.

During his time as chief justice, Warren rarely granted interviews or gave speeches. It was his view that the Supreme Court spoke through its opinions, and he stayed away from the press as much as possible. After his retirement, however, Warren hit the banquet circuit, and gave many speeches and accepted a number of awards. He also spent a lot of time enjoying outdoor pursuits such as hunting and fishing, and he often went to baseball and football games.

Warren died in Washington, D.C., at the age of eighty-three on July 9, 1974, of congestive heart failure, leaving behind a legacy as perhaps the greatest and most progressive chief justice ever to serve on the U.S. Supreme Court.

The eulogies following his death were effusive. Despite his detractors, he was recognized as a man who had altered the course of American history. *Time* magazine, in an obituary printed July 22, 1974, wrote: "When Warren died last week of heart disease at 83, the evidence was already in: during his 16 historic years as head of the Supreme Court . . . he had joined the small company of men who wrought fundamental changes in U.S. society. He had more impact on his time—and on the future—than many Presidents."

His funeral was held at Washington National Cathedral, and he was buried at Arlington National Cemetery, where his headstone is inscribed with a quote uttered by Warren in 1972:

> Where there is injustice, we should correct it. Where there is poverty, we should eliminate it. Where there is corruption, we should stamp it out. Where there is violence we should punish it. Where there is neglect, we should provide care. Where there is war, we should restore peace. And wherever corrections are achieved we should add them permanently to our storehouse of treasures.

During his lifetime Warren had his champions and detractors. But ultimately his legacy was cemented as a civil rights warrior who was ahead of his time, a man whose rulings reshaped the law and the country. He was posthumously awarded the Presidential Medal of Freedom on January 16, 1981, by President Jimmy Carter.

APPENDIX
SELECTED SUPREME COURT CASES

Brown v. Board of Education (1954)	
PLAINTIFF	**DEFENDANT**
Oliver Brown sued the Topeka, Kansas, Board of Education for sending his daughter, Linda, to an all-black segregated school when there was another school closer to their home.	The Topeka school board, which said that Linda Brown's education was equal to that received in white-only schools.
Arguments	
Segregated education is inferior to integrated education.	The facilities, curricula, and teacher's pay are equal in white and black schools.
Decision	
Brown won. The court ruled that segregation in public schools deprives children of equal protection under the law, and that separate educational facilities are inherently unequal.	

Watkins v. United States (1957)

PLAINTIFF	DEFENDANT
John T. Watkins, a labor union official, refused to answer the questions of the House Un-American Activities Committee, as to whether he or his past associates had ever been members of the Communist Party. He was convicted of contempt and appealed to the Supreme Court.	The U.S. House Un-American Activities Committee.

Arguments

Watkins said he was not given the opportunity to determine whether he was within his rights to refuse to answer the committee's questions.	Congressional committees have broad powers. As long as the committee's inquiry is legitimate and the questions are pertinent, it is not the job of the courts to interfere with the committee.

Decision

Watkins won. The Court ruled that he was denied his Fifth Amendment rights to due process.

NAACP v. Alabama (1958)

PLAINTIFF	DEFENDANT
The National Association for the Advancement of Colored People, which was found in contempt for not turning over a list of its members to the state.	The state of Alabama, which had demanded a copy of the NAACP's membership list as part of an effort to expel the group from the state for allegedly violating a business law by not registering with the state.

Arguments

Revealing the identities of members would adversely affect them and might dissuade others from joining the group for fear of the consequences.	The NAACP was in noncompliance with the state's corporate registration and business qualification laws.

Decision

The NAACP won. The Court affirmed that the constitutional rights of free speech and assembly include a right to private group association, meaning the NAACP could keep its membership information confidential.

Mapp v. Ohio (1961)

PLAINTIFF	DEFENDANT
Dollree Mapp of Cleveland, Ohio, was accused of hiding a person suspected in a bombing. Her home was searched, and while the person was not there, police found pornography and she was later convicted on that charge.	The State of Ohio Court of Appeals, representing the Cleveland Police Department.

Arguments

The Fourth Amendment, which ensures freedom from unreasonable search and seizure, was violated when police forced their way into her home without a search warrant.	The evidence (the obscene materials) was admissible in trial because it was found in a trunk, and not forcefully taken from Mapp.

Decision

Mapp won. The Court ruled that evidence obtained during a search that violates the Fourth Amendment is inadmissible in state courts.

Baker v. Carr (1962)

PLAINTIFF	DEFENDANT
Charles W. Baker of Memphis, Tennessee, and nine other voters sued to force changes in the state's election procedures.	Joe C. Carr, Secretary of State of Tennessee. He didn't draw the legislative lines, but was ultimately responsible for the actions of the state legislature, which did.

Arguments

The Tennessee constitution says electoral districts should be changed every ten years, but it hadn't been done since 1901, resulting in the votes of rural citizens being worth more than those of voters living in urban areas.	Legislative districts and apportionment are political questions, and the courts shouldn't be involved.

Decision

Baker won. The justices said if a state lets one person's vote count for more than another's because they are in different districts, then the state is denying its citizens equal protection of the laws.

Engel v. Vitale (1962)

PLAINTIFF	DEFENDANT
Steven I. Engel and four other parents of students in New York public schools wanted a school-mandated prayer discontinued.	William J. Vitale Jr. and other members of the board of education.

Arguments

If government may regulate or require religious practice in public school, then it gains power over matters that should be free.	Prayer gives moral training for good citizenship.

Decision

Engel won. The court ruled that compelling students to pray in school was unconstitutional, and no government should compose official prayers for Americans to recite.

Gideon v. Wainwright (1963)

PLAINTIFF	DEFENDANT
Clarence Earl Gideon, accused of breaking into a pool hall in Florida, tried to get a court-appointed lawyer but failed. He persuaded the Supreme Court to review his case.	Louie L. Wainwright, secretary to the Florida Department of Corrections.

Arguments

Without a lawyer, no man may get the fair trial the Sixth Amendment demands.	The issue should be left to each state to decide, and states should be given a fair amount of latitude in deciding what constitutes a fair trial.

Decision

Gideon won. The justices agreed that no one should have to defend himself against a felony charge, trying to understand laws he never read. If a defendant has no money for a lawyer, the state must appoint one for him.

N.Y. Times v. Sullivan (1964)

PLAINTIFF	DEFENDANT
The *New York Times*, which ran a full-page ad alleging that the arrest of the Rev. Martin Luther King, Jr. in Alabama was part of a campaign to destroy King's efforts in favor of integration and voting rights.	L.B. Sullivan, Montgomery city commissioner, who sued the newspaper and the four black ministers who endorsed the ad for libel, claiming he was personally defamed.

Arguments	
Sullivan's lawsuit infringed on the newspaper's First Amendment right to freedom of speech and freedom of the press.	Under Alabama law, Sullivan did not have to prove he'd been personally harmed by the ad.

Decision	
The newspaper won. The Court found that the First Amendment protects publication of all statements about the conduct of public officials, even false ones, as long as they are made without actual knowledge that the statements are false.	

Miranda v. Arizona (1966)

PLAINTIFF	DEFENDANT
Ernesto Miranda, who was arrested in Phoenix and convicted of kidnapping and rape after he confessed to the crime.	The State of Arizona.

Arguments	
The arresting officers did not inform Miranda of his Fifth Amendment right against self-incrimination, or his Sixth Amendment right to have an attorney. So even though he confessed, his confession should have been excluded from the trial.	Miranda confessed to the crime, and did not specifically request an attorney. Having to inform all suspects of their constitutional rights would undermine the efficiency of the police.

Decision	
Miranda won. The Court ruled that the police had not taken the proper steps to inform Miranda of his rights.	

Loving v. Virginia (1967)

PLAINTIFF	DEFENDANT
Richard Loving, a white man, who married Mildred Jeter, a black woman. They were sentenced to a year in prison for getting married in another state, and then moving to Virginia.	The state of Virginia, which accused them of violating the state law forbidding interracial marriage.

Arguments

The state law violates the equal protection clause of the Fourteenth Amendment.	God did not intend for the races to mix, and their Fourteenth Amendment rights to equal protection were not violated because both Loving and his wife were punished equally.

Decision

Loving won. The Court found the Virginia law had no purpose other than racial discrimination.

In re: Gault (1967)

PLAINTIFF	DEFENDANT
Gerald Francis Gault, age 15, who was arrested for allegedly making an obscene phone call.	The Arizona Supreme Court and the sheriff of Gila County, Arizona, who arrested Gault after a neighbor complained of receiving a lewd phone call.

Arguments

Gault's parents, who were at work at the time, should have been notified of his arrest because he is a minor. His parents were not allowed to see him, he was not advised of his right to an attorney, nor did the victim ever testify – all constitutional violations.	The purpose of juvenile court should be correction, not punishment, so the constitutional procedural safeguards for adult criminal trials should not apply.

Decision

Gault won. The Court ruled the police and courts had violated his due process rights, guaranteed by the Fourth Amendment, and that juveniles are entitled to the same due process rights as adults.

TIMELINE

1891 Born on March 19 in Los Angeles, California.

1912 Graduates from U.C. Berkeley with a bachelor's degree in legal studies.

1914 Earns bachelor of law degree from Boalt Hall law school; admitted to the state bar.

1917 Enlists in the U.S. Army during World War I.

1918 Discharged from the Army with the rank of first lieutenant.

1920 Becomes deputy city attorney for the city of Oakland.

1925 Marries Swedish-born widow Nina Elisabeth Palmquist; becomes Alameda County district attorney.

1938 Elected attorney general of California.

1942 Elected governor of California, beating Democratic incumbent.

1947 Signs law repealing school segregation statutes in California.

1948   Accepts Republican vice presidential nomination on a ticket with Thomas Dewey.

1953   Appointed to the U.S. Supreme Court, and becomes the fourteenth chief justice; decides *Brown v. Board of Education*, banning segregation in public schools.

1963   *Gideon v. Wainwright* case holds that indigent criminal defendants are entitled to publicly-funded counsel.

1964   The Warren Commission issues its report on its investigation into the assassination of President John Kennedy.

1966   *Miranda v. Arizona* decision requires that rights of a person being interrogated by police be clearly explained.

1969   Retires from the U.S. Supreme Court.

1974   Dies at age eighty-three in Washington, D.C.

1981   Posthumously awarded the Presidential Medal of Freedom.

Sources

CHAPTER ONE:
A SON OF SCANDINAVIA

p. 11   "My boy, when you were born . . ." Ed Cray, *Chief Justice: A Biography of Earl Warren* (New York: Simon & Schuster, 1997), 17.

p. 11   "was the biggest damn fool . . ." Earl Warren, *The Memoirs of Chief Justice Earl Warren* (Garden City, N.Y.: Doubleday, 1977), 5.

p. 12   "My years on the Court . . ." Ibid., 7.

p. 13   "pedigree established . . ." Ibid., 15.

p. 13   "This seemed a bit pompous . . ." Ibid.

p. 14   "The Lord must have . . ." Ibid., 24.

p. 16   "You cuss it . . ." Ibid., 22.

p. 17   "I witnessed crime . . ." Ibid., 30-31.

p. 17   "The things I learned . . ." Ibid., 31.

CHAPTER TWO:
A LEGAL CAREER INTERRUPTED

p. 19   "Well, my boy . . ." Warren, *The Memoirs of Chief Justice Earl Warren*, 32.

p. 20   "sad sight . . ." Ibid., 34.

p. 20   "I must admit . . ." Ibid., 36.

p. 21   "It was a whole new world . . ." Ibid.

p. 21   "All of this may sound . . ." Ibid., 41.

p. 22   "I have had probably fifty . . ." Ibid., 45.

p. 24   "It was exciting . . ." Ibid., 61-62.

CHAPTER THREE:
MARRIAGE AND FAMILY

p. 28   "atrocious." Warren, *The Memoirs of Chief Justice Earl Warren,* 65.

p. 29   "Nina, the best thing . . ." Ibid., v.

CHAPTER FOUR:
A SUCCESSFUL PROSECUTOR

p. 32   "It was never the culprit . . ." Warren, *The Memoirs of Chief Justice Earl Warren*, 119.

p. 35   "If the Japs . . ." Alden Whitman, "Earl Warren, 83, Who Led High Court In Time of Vast Social Change, Is Dead." *New York Times*, July 10, 1974, http://www.nytimes.com/learning/general/onthisday/0319.html, 9.

p. 35   "I have since deeply regretted . . ." Warren, *The Memoirs of Chief Justice Earl Warren*, 149.

CHAPTER FIVE:
A POPULAR GOVERNOR

p. 38   "I believed then . . ." Warren, *The Memoirs of Chief Justice Earl Warren*, 187.

CHAPTER SIX:
SUPER CHIEF

p. 44   "almost bombastically pretentious . . ." Supreme Court Historical Society, "Home of the Court." http://www.supremecourthistory.org/history/supremecourthistory_history_homes.htm.

p. 44   "It is indeed an awesome . . ." Warren, *The Memoirs of Chief Justice Earl Warren*, 1.

p. 46   "The writer of the letter . . ." Dwight D. Eisenhower, "The Presidential Papers of Dwight David Eisenhower, Vo. XIV: Document #460; Oct. 9, 1953, Personal and confidential to Milton Stover Eisenhower." http://www.eisenhowermemorial.org/presidential-papers/first-term/documents/460.cfm.

p. 47 "But he was an instinctive . . ." Bernard Schwartz, *Super Chief, Earl Warren and his Supreme Court—A Judicial Biography* (New York: New York University Press, 1983), 31.

p. 47 "(He was) physically . . ." William J. Brennan, Jr. "Chief Justice Warren." *Harvard Law Review* 88, no. 1 (November 1974): 1.

p. 48 "a mild and genial . . ." Alden Whitman, "Earl Warren, 83, Who Led High Court In Time of Vast Social Change, Is Dead."

CHAPTER SEVEN:
AN END TO SEGREGATION

p. 52 "In Brown the key . . ." Street Law, Inc. "Landmark Cases of the U.S. Supreme Court: Brown v. Board of Education, Mapp v. Ohio, Gideon v. Wainwright, Miranda v. Arizona." http://www.streetlaw.org/en/Case.6/aspx.

p. 53 "Contrary to speculations . . ." Warren, *The Memoirs of Chief Justice Earl Warren*, 2.

p. 53 "As we Justices . . ." Ibid., 3.

p. 53 "Segregation of white . . ." Earl Warren, Unanimous opinion in Brown v. Board of Education, 1954. Accessed via http://www.milestonedocuments.com/documents/full-text/brown-v-board-of-education.

P. 54 "I read: "We come . . ." Warren, *The Memoirs of Chief Justice Earl Warren*, 3.

p. 54 "I do not think . . ." The Library of Congress. "Notes, William O. Douglas to Earl Warren, 11 May 1954; Harold H. Burton to Warren, 17 May 1954; and Felix Frankfurter to Warren, 17 May 1954, concerning Chief Justice Warren's decision in Brown v. Board of Education." http://memory.loc.gov/mss/mcc/052/0001.jpg.

p. 54   "Today I believe . . ." Ibid.

p. 55   "This is a day . . ." Ibid.

CHAPTER EIGHT:
A NATION CHANGES

P. 60   "People do misinterpret . . ." Warren, *The Memoirs of Chief Justice Earl Warren*, 4.

P. 60   "It has been written . . ." Ibid., 4-5.

p. 61   "I do not see how . . ." Whitman, "Earl Warren, 83, Who Led High Court In Time of Vast Social Change, Is Dead."

p. 61   "dangerous and subversive . . ." Cray, *Chief Justice: A Biography of Earl Warren.*

p. 61   "I never took any . . ." Transcript, Earl Warren Oral History Interview I, Sept. 21, 1971, by Joe B. Frantz, Lyndon Baines Johnson Library and Museum. http://www.lbjlib.utexas.edu/johnson/archives.hom/oralhistory.hom/Warren-E/Warren-E.asp, 4.

CHAPTER NINE:
YOU HAVE THE RIGHT TO REMAIN SILENT

p. 65   "Comes now the petitioner . . ." Supreme Court Historical Society Web site. "The Warren Court, 1953-1969." http://www.supremecourthistory.org/history/supremecourthistory_history_history_warren.htm, 2.

p. 66   "If an obscure . . ." Paul C. Reardon, and James Vorenberg. "The New England Defender Conference: A Brief Report." *Boston University Law Review* XLIV, no. 1 (winter 1964).

CHAPTER TEN:
ONE MAN, ONE VOTE

p. 72 "Legislators represent people, . . ." Earl Warren, Majority opinion in Reynolds v. Sims, 1964. Accessed via http://www.milestonedocuments. com/documents/full-text/earl-warrens-opinion-in-reynolds-v-sims/.

p. 72 "These decisions give support . . ." Ibid.

p.72XX "Every man's judgment . . ." Transcript, Earl Warren Oral History Interview I, 24.

p. 73 "Almost every important decision . . ." Ibid., 8.

p. 73 "I think in the past . . ." Ibid.

p. 73 "Mr. Warren's Court . . ." Whitman, "Earl Warren, 83, Who Led High Court In Time of Vast Social Change, Is Dead."

CHAPTER ELEVEN:
THE WARREN COMMISSION

p. 76 "in a temporary fit . . ." Report of the President's Commission on the Assassination of President John F. Kennedy (Washington, DC: United States Government Printing Office, 1964), 17.

p. 77 "Practically all of us . . ." Transcript, Earl Warren Oral History Interview I, 11.

p. 77 "The President told me . . ." Ibid.

p. 77 "McNamara had told him . . ." Ibid.

p. 77 "This thing is of . . ." Ibid.

p. 78 "the unhappiest time . . ." Whitman, "Earl Warren, 83, Who Led High Court In Time of Vast Social Change, Is Dead."

p. 78 "The only reason . . ." Ibid.

p. 78 "The assassination of John . . ." Report of the President's Commission on the Assassination of President John F. Kennedy, 1.

p. 78   "in recognition of the right . . ." Ibid.

p. 78   "showed disdain for democracy . . ." Ibid., 13.

p. 79   "very persuasive evidence . . ." Ibid., 19.

p. 80   "Because of the difficulty . . ." Ibid., 22.

p. 80   "The numerous statements . . ." Ibid., 20.

p. 81   "While the Commission . . ." Edward Jay Epstein, "Who's Afraid of the Warren Report." *Esquire*, December, 1966. http://www.edwardjayepstein. com/archived/warrenreport.htm, 2.

p. 82   "had never been satisfied . . ." Transcript, Earl Warren Oral History Interview I, 18.

p. 83   "The Warren Commission . . ." "Epstein, "Who's Afraid of the Warren Report."

p. 83   "This phenomenon . . ." Ibid.

p. 84   "I was satisfied . . ." Transcript, Earl Warren Oral History Interview I, op.cit., 15.

p. 84   "demented people," Ibid., 16.

p. 84   "I occasionally see . . ." Ibid. 19.

CHAPTER TWELVE:
FINAL YEARS

p. 87   "President Johnson, when . . ." Transcript, Earl Warren Oral History Interview I, 5.

p. 88   "I would like the Court . . ." Whitman, "Earl Warren, 83, Who Led High Court In Time of Vast Social Change, Is Dead."

p. 89   "When Warren died . . ." Unknown author. "The Law: Earl Warren's Way: Is It Fair?" *Time*, July 22, 1974. http://www.time.com/time/ printout/0,8816,942946,00.html.

p. 89   "Where there is injustice . . ." Arlington National Cemetery Web site. "Earl Warren, First Lieutenant, United States Army, Governor of California, Chief Justice of the United States Supreme Court." http:// www.arlingtoncemetery.net/ewarren.htm.

BIBLIOGRAPHY

Allen, Anita L. "NAACP v. Alabama, Privacy and Data Protection." NAACP Web site (June 27, 2008). http://naacpvalabamaat50.org/.

Arlington National Cemetery Web site. "Earl Warren, First Lieutenant, United States Army, Governor of California, Chief Justice of the United States Supreme Court." http://www.arlingtoncemetery.net/ewarren.htm.

Ariens, Michael. "Supreme Court Justices: Earl Warren (1891-1974)." http://www.michaelariens.com/ConLaw/justices/warren.htm. C. 2002-2005.

Brennan, William J., Jr. "Chief Justice Warren." *Harvard Law Review* 88, no. 1 (November 1974): 1.

Cray, Ed. *Chief Justice: A Biography of Earl Warren.* New York: Simon & Schuster, 1997.

Eisenhower, Dwight D. "The Presidential Papers of Dwight David Eisenhower, Vo. XIV: Document #460; Oct. 9, 1953, Personal and confidential to Milton Stover Eisenhower." http://www.eisenhowermemorial.org/presidential-papers/first-term/documents/460.cfm.

Epstein, Edward Jay. "Who's Afraid of the Warren Report." *Esquire*, December, 1966. http://www.edwardjayepstein.com/archived/warrenreport.htm.

Federal Judicial Center Web site. "Biographical Directory of Federal Judges: Warren, Earl." http://www.fjc.gov/servlet/nGetInfo?jid=2506&cid=999&ctype=na&instate=na.

FindLaw Supreme Court Center Web site. "Earl Warren." http://supreme.lp.findlaw.com/supreme_court/justices/pastjustices/warren.html.

Harrison, Maureen, and Steve Gilbert, eds. *Landmark Decisions of the Supreme Court VI.* San Diego, Calif.: Excellent Books, 1999.

Hutchinson, Dennis J. "Hail to the Chief: Earl Warren and the Supreme Court." *Michigan Law Review* 81, no. 4 (March 1983): 922-930.

The Library of Congress Web site. "Notes, William O. Douglas to Earl Warren, 11 May 1954; Harold H. Burton to Warren, 17 May 1954; and Felix Frankfurter to Warren, 17 May 1954, concerning Chief Justice Warren's decision in Brown v. Board of Education." http://memory.loc.gov/mss/mcc/052/0001.jpg.

Newton, Jim. *Justice For All: Earl Warren and the Nation He Made.* New York: Riverhead Books, 2006.

The McGraw-Hill Encyclopedia of World Biography, Vol. 11, *Earl Warren.* Ann Arbor, Mich.: The University of Michigan, McGraw-Hill, 1973.

Powe, Lucas A., Jr. *The Warren Court and American Politics.* Cambridge, Mass.: The Belknap Press of Harvard University Press, 2000.

Reardon, Paul C. and James Vorenberg. "The New England Defender Conference: A Brief Report." *Boston University Law Review* XLIV, no. 1 (winter 1964).

Report of the President's Commission on the Assassination of President John F. Kennedy, Washington, DC: United States Government Printing Office, 1964. http://www.archives.gov/research/jfk/warren-commission-report/index.html.

Schwartz, Bernard. *Super Chief, Earl Warren and his Supreme Court—A Judicial Biography.* New York: New York University Press, 1983.

———. and Stephan Lesher. *Inside the Warren Court, 1953-1969.* Garden City, N.Y.: Doubleday, 1983.

Street Law, Inc. Web site. "Earl Warren Biography." http://www.streetlaw.org//en/Page.Landmark.Brown.bio.warren.aspx.

————. "Landmark Cases of the U.S. Supreme Court. *Brown v. Board of Education*, *Mapp v. Ohio*, *Gideon V. Wainwright*, *Miranda v. Arizona*.

Supreme Court Historical Society Web site. "Home of the Court." http://www.supremecourthistory.org/history/supremecourthistory_history_homes.htm

Supreme Court Historical Society Web site. "The Warren Court, 1953-1969." http://www.supremecourthistory.org/history/supremecourthistory_history_history_warren.htm.

Transcript, Earl Warren Oral History Interview I, Sept. 21, 1971, by Joe B. Frantz, Lyndon Baines Johnson Library and Museum. http://www.lbjlib.utexas.edu/johnson/archives.hom/oralhistory.hom/Warren-E/Warren-E.asp.

Unknown author. "The Law: Earl Warren's Way: Is It Fair?" *Time*, July 22, 1974. http://www.time.com/time/printout/0,8816,942946,00.html.
U.S. History.com Web site. "Earl Warren." http://www.u-s-history.com/pages/h3834.html.

Warren, Earl. *The Memoirs of Chief Justice Earl Warren*. Garden City, N.Y.: Doubleday, 1977.

————. Unanimous opinion in *Brown v. Board of Education*, 1954. http://www.milestonedocuments.com/documents/full-text/brown-v-board-of-education.

————. Majority opinion in *Reynolds v. Sims*, 1964. http://www.milestonedocuments.com/documents/full-text/earl-warrens-opinion-in-reynolds-v-sims/.

Weaver, John D. *Warren: The Man, The Court, The Era*. Boston, Mass.: Little, Brown, 1967.

Whitman, Alden. "Earl Warren, 83, Who Led High Court In Time of Vast Social Change, Is Dead." *New York Times*, July 10, 1974. http://www.nytimes.com/learning/general/onthisday/0319.html.

WEB SITES

HTTP://WWW.HISTORYOFSUPREMECOURT.ORG

Written for educators and students, this site contains information about the history of the U.S. Supreme Court and major Supreme Court decisions, broken down by topic, including basic rights, gender and young people. It also contains essays, images and interactive exercises.

HTTP://WWWSUPREMECOURTHISTORY.ORG

The Web site of the Supreme Court Historical Society, established for the purpose of expanding public awareness of the history and heritage of the Court. It contains the full history of the Supreme Court and information on how the court works.

HTTP://WWW.SUPREMECOURT.GOV

The Web site of the Supreme Court of the United States, it contains current information on justices, opinions, arguments, recent decisions, speeches and reports.

HTTP://WWW.FJC.GOV/HISTORY/JUDGES.HTML

A page on the Web site of the Federal Judicial Center, which contains a biographical directory of all federal judges since 1789, plus information on judicial history, landmark legislation and historic courthouses.

HTTP://BANCROFT.BERKELEY.EDU/ROHO/PROJECTS/EWGE/

The Earl Warren Era Project (a project of the Bancroft Library at the University of California, Berkeley) documents the executive branch, the legislature, criminal justice, and political campaigns during the Warren Era in California. Focusing on the years 1925-1953, the interviews also provide a record of the life of Earl Warren.

HTTP://WWW.CALIFORNIAGOVERNORS.CA.GOV/H/BIOGRAPHY/
GOVERNOR_30HTML#ADMINISTRATION

California's governors are featured on this site, and here you'll find a short biography of Warren, the thirtieth governor of California, and his three inaugural addresses.

HTTP://WWW.LBJLIB.UTEXAS.EDU/JOHNSON/ARCHIVES.HOM/
ORALHISTORY.HOM/WARREN-E/WARREN-E.ASP

A September 21, 1971, interview with Earl Warren on the role of the Supreme Court and the Warren Commission on the assassination of John Kennedy is detailed here, on the site of the Lyndon Baines Johnson Library and Museum.

INDEX

CREDITS